# Sound School
# Finance for
# Educational Excellence

# Sound School Finance for Educational Excellence

Stephen Coffin and Bruce S. Cooper

ROWMAN & LITTLEFIELD
Lanham • Boulder • New York • London

Published by Rowman & Littlefield
A wholly owned subsidiary of The Rowman & Littlefield Publishing Group, Inc.
4501 Forbes Boulevard, Suite 200, Lanham, Maryland 20706
www.rowman.com

Unit A, Whitacre Mews, 26-34 Stannary Street, London SE11 4AB

**British Library Cataloguing-in-Publication Information Available**

**Library of Congress Cataloging-in-Publication Data Available**

978-1-4758-3819-0 (cloth : alk. paper)
978-1-4758-3820-6 (pbk. : alk. paper)
978-1-4758-3821-3 (electronic)

♾️™ The paper used in this publication meets the minimum requirements of American National Standard for Information Sciences—Permanence of Paper for Printed Library Materials, ANSI/NISO Z39.48-1992.

Printed in the United States of America

# Contents

# Foreword

In times such as the present, when resources for public education are increasingly harder to come by—and remaining static at best, if they are not decreasing—it is incumbent on educational leaders at all levels in K-12 schools, especially principals, to have a good working knowledge of the ins-and-outs of school finance. It is important for principals to understand the various sources from which school revenues are derived, how they are managed, and how they are spent.

Whether in traditional schools or in districts moving to site-based models of management—as well as emerging new forms of public education such as charter schools—the focus in this useful book is on principals because they are in the best position to assess the needs of the schools, and students, they serve.

Aware of the need for line educators, such as principals, to understand the basics of school finance, this volume, *Sound District Finance for Educational Excellence*, is edited by Bruce S. Cooper, an emeritus professor at Fordham University, and Steven Coffin, a PhD candidate, who serves as an adjunct faculty member at Fordham and who teaches courses on school finance. Cooper has spent much of his career focusing on issues of finance and equity designed to provide quality educational programs for all children that is a breath of fresh air for practitioners.

In an area that can quickly devolve into a hodgepodge of virtually impenetrable jargon, *Finance Leadership for Excellence in Schools* is written in an easy-to-read, nontechnical language accessible to practitioners and academicians alike.

To understand its importance to educators, it is worth keeping in mind that the field, now known as School Finance, burst into prominence on the national legal scene in 1971. For in 1971, the opinion of the Supreme Court

vii

of California in *Serrano v. Priest* generated more reaction than any other state court case on school finance, perhaps, in history. At the core of *Serrano I* was the court's view that California's funding scheme, which rendered the quality of a child's education dependent on a local school district's wealth, invidiously discriminated against the poor—in violation of the Equal Protection Clause of the Fourteenth Amendment of the U.S. Constitution, as well as many state constitutions.

The court held that insofar as the wealth of districts was the basis for substantially different per-pupil expenditures (as reflected by examples of school systems with high property values which, with low tax rates, spent much more per child than others with high tax rates and lower property valuations), the system was unconstitutional and had to be reformed.

Four years later, in *San Antonio Independent School District v. Rodriguez* (San Antonio, Texas), in its only case on the merits of school finance, the U.S. Supreme Court essentially repudiated the approach taken by the Supreme Court of California. In an often-quoted language, the Court reasoned that "[e]ducation, of course, is not among the rights afforded explicit protection under our Federal Constitution. Nor do we find any basis for saying it is implicitly so protected." The Supreme Court's refusal to apply the U.S. Constitution to disputes over school finance means that since *San Antonio*, litigation on the essential topics is all but virtually exclusive the focus of *state*, rather than federal, courts.

Two years later, however, in the first of what would become a multitude of state school finance cases, the Supreme Court of California distinguished its case from *San Antonio*, reaffirming its initial judgment pursuant to the state constitution in *Serrano v. Priest II*. In the years since *Serrano v. Priest II*, litigation has occurred in virtually every state, challenging state funding formulas. This near-avalanche of litigation is almost evenly split as plaintiffs have succeeded in about half of the states where they challenged systems of school funding. In light of this steady stream of change over the nature of school funding in various states, *Sound District Finance for Educational Excellence* should be an indispensable guide for principals and other educational leaders at all levels in K-12 educational systems.

Written by a wide array of scholar-practitioners with a breadth of experience in a variety of educational settings, the chapters in *Sound District Finance for Educational Excellence* offer a hands-on analysis on the key topic in today's world of school finance. Starting with the concept of value to help taxpayers, educators, and ultimately students achieve excellence in education, this volume is divided into fifteen far-ranging topics. Following a discussion of the issue of value, the book reviews such timely issues.

Budgeting and various models to accomplish quality finance in schools are important tasks, particularly in relation to divergent student populations, to the place of leadership in achieving equitable finance to the key role of personnel.

*Sound District Finance for Educational Excellence* also reviews such timely issues as: (1) those costs associated with special education; (2) working with federal, state, and local aid; and (3) contentious issues surrounding privatization, vouchers, religious school education, tuition tax credits; and charter schools. The book rounds out with a chapter on the crucial issue of law before ending with the editors' thoughts about moving forward in improving the financing of public education to achieve excellence, especially for improving student learning outcomes.

In sum, *Sound District Finance for Educational Excellence* is a most welcomed addition to the literature in the field as it provides thought-provoking suggestions, along with hands-on information, for improving the way money gets to and is spent in schools, designed to provide excellence in education for all children. One can only hope that readers will take to heart the lessons contained in this readable volume by providing value in education for all students.

Charles J. Russo, JD, EdD

# Introduction and Value Proposition

## Bruce S. Cooper and Stephen Coffin

Quality school finance is integral to the funding and provision of a full, adequate education for all. Indeed, a school district's budget is the financial representation of its educational purposes and plans. Thus, a clarion alert for all teachers: "If it's not in your *budget*, it won't be in your *classroom* for your students and for you."

However, sound school finance is increasingly challenging in an era of higher educational needs and scarcer resources. This book—as it provides an in-depth understanding of fundamental practices, processes, and lessons learned—not only benefits all school administrators, personnel, parents, students, and other stakeholders, but it also undergirds the provision of an excellent education.

This book focuses on key building blocks essential for the provision of an excellent education. The value proposition inherent in this book should work well for all schools, districts, students, and school stakeholders regardless of location, size, type, and demographic mix. The components of sound school finance that are increasingly important in an era of scarce financial, material, and human resources include but are not limited to the following.

These are the topics that school administrators, teachers, and personnel; and scholars, professors, and parents and the education world want and need. Current market offerings do not meet their preferences! As a PhD candidate in education, adjunct professor of school finance, full emeritus professor, and former school business administrator, we the editors and authors believe that we have a grand opportunity for a successful and meaningful book for school leaders.

Thus, the nation is keeping its eyes on its schools—including their programs, staff, funding, and students' results. Yet a readable, practical handbook on how best to finance and budget in these schools was not available.

Everyone is affected as follows: (1) principals must raise the money and make the resources work for their students; (2) teachers need good pay and benefits, plus better equipment, technology, and materials—and support in their classrooms; and (3) students must learn and benefit from the educational experience. And school systems need to use public funds efficiently—and equitably and effectively—if education and kids are to succeed.

For example, "The number of states that mandate principals' evaluations has jumped in recent years, driven by rules tying federal education aid to such policies. But many districts are still grappling with the best ways to measure principal effectiveness—and the extent to which students' performance should be included in evaluating principals."

Since 2010, at least thirty-six states have adopted laws requiring principals to undergo regular assessments and increasing the rigor of those reviews, according to the National Conference of State Legislatures. The changes reflect a shift from largely pro forma evaluations to complicated matrices that seek to tie principals' effectiveness, in part, to students' academic growth. The policies typically require that a percentage of a principal's evaluation include students' performance and/or growth. The amount ranges, for example, from 20 percent in Delaware to 50 percent of the overall score in states such as Georgia and Ohio.

We realize just how important communications and good professional relations are for leaders to develop in their schools. For as Daly explains, "Relationships are central for the retention, increased professionalism, and depth of engagement of educators" (Daly, 2010, p. 1).

This book does the trick, as we explore the sources, the most effective and efficient uses of funds, and what school leaders must do to get the "most for their money" in organizing, supporting, providing, and overseeing a quality school. We connect the four corners of the process that include the *Funding, Leadership, Programs*, and *Outcomes*. We take a systems approach: starting with the "INPUTS"—the teachers, other staff, materials, and program; we then have chapters on the "*THROUGH-PUTS*," including instruction, bidding, and purchasing, and the "*OUTPUTS*," that include "the three-G's" of education—students' *grades, growth*, and *graduation rates*.

Principals are the key school leaders in the process; but they cannot do it without the latest methods, knowledge, and technology, which this book provides.

The nation is keeping its eyes on its schools—including their programs, staff, funding, and students' results and importantly, particularly on school funding from all sources and levels. Yet a readable, practical handbook on how best to finance, budget, and spend valuable dollars in these schools is not available. Everyone is affected: principals must raise the money and make the resources work for their students; teachers need good pay and benefits, plus better equipment, technology, and materials—and support. And school systems need to use public funds efficiently—and equitably and effectively—if education and students are to succeed.

Superville (2014) reminds us just how important good leadership is at the school site, where students, teachers, and specialists work together using available funds and other resources. And we are seeing that, now, more and more jurisdictions evaluating principals in their fiscal management abilities.

But many are still grappling with the best ways to measure principal effectiveness and the extent to which student performance should be included in evaluating principals" (Superville, 2014, p. 14).

Since 2010, at least thirty-six states have adopted laws requiring principals to undergo regular assessments, and increasing the rigor of those reviews, according to the National Conference of State Legislatures. The changes reflect a shift from largely pro forma evaluations to complicated matrices that seek to tie principals' effectiveness, in part, to students' academic growth. The policies typically require that a percentage of a principal's evaluation include students' performance and/or growth. The amount ranges, for example, from 20 percent in Delaware to 50 percent of the overall score in states such as Georgia and Ohio.

This book does the trick, as we explore the financial sources, the most effective and efficient uses of funds, and what school leaders must do to get the "most for their money" in organizing, supporting, and overseeing a quality school. We connect the four corners of the process that include the *Funding, Leadership, Programs*, and *Outcomes*.

And, we take a systems approach: (1) starting with the "INPUTS"—the teachers, other staff, materials, funds, and program; (2) we then have chapters on the "*THROUGH-PUTS*," including instruction, bidding, and purchasing; and (3) the "*OUTPUTS*," that include "the three-G's" of education—students' grades, growth, and graduation rates.

Principals are thus the key leaders in the process, but they cannot do it without the latest methods, knowledge and technology, which this book provides.

## REFERENCES

Daly, A. J. (Ed.). *Social network theory and educational change* (pp. 179–96). Cambridge, MA: Harvard Education Press.

Superville, D. R. (May 20, 2014 online; in print, December 28, 2016). "States Forge Ahead on Principal Evaluation," *Education Week*, pp. 32–33.

*Section I*

# VALUE PROPOSITION

*Chapter 1*

# FOUR "E" Words of Quality School Finance

## *Equity, Equality, Efficiency, and Effectiveness*

### Bruce S. Cooper and Stephen Coffin

The four key "E-words" in education, equity, equality, efficiency, and effectiveness, are heard ringing in our schools in the United States, as judges, presidents (yes, President Donald Trump), school boards, and superintendents—not to mention teachers, parents, and citizens—use these terms when describing the funding, process, and outcomes of education. As the president said recently of the federal role in funding schools, as National Public Radio reported in "Trump's Plan for Education" (September 2016):

> Those services include providing roughly $15 billion in Title I funds to help schools that educate at-risk students, more than $12 billion for students with special needs, and some $29 billion in Pell Grants to help low-income students pay for college. (All according to 2016 Congressional appropriations)

School leaders need to understand the terms, *efficiency* and *effectiveness*, plus *equity* and *equality,* including their (1) similarities, (2) differences, and (3) uses, and even their (4) misuses—and misunderstandings of them. This chapter defines and explains these terms and ideas and works to relate them to the financing and improvement of schools.

### TERM 1: EFFECTIVENESS

Let's start with, perhaps, the most obvious, and vital of the E-words, *Effectiveness*, since everyone in every nation wants schools to be better, and more *effective*. As one international study explains in "How did the world's best-performing school systems come out on top!":

> We examine what these high-performing school systems have in common and what tools they use to improve student outcomes. The experiences of these top school systems suggests that three things matter most: (1) getting the right people to become teachers, (2) developing them into effective instructors and, (3) ensuring that the system is able to deliver the best possible instruction for every child. (Eichhorn of McKinsey Company, September 2007, p. 31)

John Eichhorn has put a useful finger on school "effectiveness" when he identified three key parts of the process: the people, the process, and the outcomes. All schools leaders want and need to be *effective* in their work and schools. As one definition explains:

> In the most general sense, "school effectiveness" refers to the level of goal attainment of a school. Although average achievement scores in core subjects, established at the end of a fixed program are the most probable "school effects," alternative criteria like the responsiveness of the school to the community and the satisfaction of the teachers may also be considered. (Eichhorn, 2007, p. 33)

Thus, *effective* means bringing students and staff up to standards, and helping students to attain a quality education and to show their ability on tests and other evaluations. McTighe and O'Connor (2004, pp. 10–17) provide six critical "practices" that help to make teachers and their students both more effective:

Practice 1: Use summative assessments to frame meaningful performance goals. To avoid the danger of viewing the standards and benchmarks simply as inert content to "cover," educators should frame the standards and benchmarks in terms of desired performances and ensure that the performances are as authentic as possible. Teachers should then present the summative performance assessment tasks to students at the beginning of a new unit or course.

**Practice 2: Show criteria and models in advance**. Unlike selected-response or short-answer tests, authentic performance assessments are typically open-ended and do not yield a single, correct answer or solution process. . . . A rubric [see Cooper and Gargan, 2009] is a widely used evaluation tool consisting of criteria, a measurement scale (a 4-point scale, for example), and descriptions of the characteristics for each score point. Well-developed rubrics communicate the important dimensions, or elements of quality, in a product or performance and guide educators in evaluating student work.

In addition, when students study and compare examples ranging in quality—from very strong to very weak—they are better able to internalize the differences. The models enable students to more accurately self-assess and improve their work before turning it in to the teacher.

**Practice 3: Assess before teaching**. Diagnostic assessment is as important to teaching as a physical exam is to prescribing an appropriate medical treatment or regimen. At the outset of any unit of study, certain students are likely to have already mastered some of the skills that the teacher is about to introduce, and others may already understand key concepts. . . . Armed with this diagnostic information, a teacher gains greater insight into what to teach, by knowing what skill gaps to address or by skipping material previously mastered; into how to teach, by using grouping options and initiating activities based on preferred learning styles and interests; and into how to connect the content to students' interests and talents. (See Shute & Cooper, 2015, on in-school truancy and cutting classes.)

**Practice 4: Offer appropriate choices**. Assessment becomes responsive when students are given appropriate options for demonstrating knowledge, skills, and understanding. Allow choices—but always with the intent of collecting needed and appropriate evidence based on goals. In the example of the 4th grade museum display project, the teacher wants students to demonstrate their understanding of the relationship between geography and economy. This could be accomplished through a newspaper article, a concept web, a PowerPoint presentation, a comparison chart, or a simulated radio interview with an expert. Learners often put forth greater effort and produce higher-quality work when given such a variety of choices. The teacher will judge these products using a three-trait rubric that focuses on accuracy of content, clarity and thoroughness of explanation, and overall product quality.

**Practice 5: Provide feedback early and often**. And, remember, the learners need opportunities to act on the feedback—to understand, refine, revise, practice, and try again. Writers rarely compose a perfect manuscript on the first try, which is why the writing process stresses cycles of drafting, feedback, and revision as the route to excellence. Not surprisingly, the best feedback often surfaces in the performance-based subjects—such as art, music, and physical education—and in extracurricular activities, such as band and athletics. Indeed, the essence of coaching involves ongoing assessment and feedback.

**Practice 6: Encourage self-assessment and goal setting**. Some examples: before turning in their science lab reports, students review their work against a list of explicit criteria. On the basis of their self-assessments, a number of students make revisions to improve their reports before handing them in. Their teacher observes that the overall quality of the lab reports has improved. The most effective learners set personal learning goals, employ proven strategies, and self-assess their work. Teachers help cultivate such habits of mind by modeling self-assessment and goal setting and by expecting students to apply these habits regularly (McTighe and O'Connor, 2004)

## TERM 2: EFFICIENCY

The next E-word is "efficiency," that is, getting the most "outputs" for the least (or right) "inputs." In many ways, financial efficiency is a ratio between funding "inputs" into an educational program or project, quality, and success of "throughputs," and the funding "outputs" or accomplishments, learning, and often through test results, outcomes, or other personal "results" (Molinar, 2014). As one study found:

> The U.S. ranks 19th out of 30 countries in the outcomes it gets from its investments in education, according to "The Efficiency Index: Which education systems deliver the best value for the money?," a report released by GEMS Education Solutions, a London-based education consultancy. (Molinar, 2014, p. 1)

In contrast, Finland, Korea, and the Czech Republic were deemed the most *educationally efficient* countries in the study, which was based on fifteen years of data from members of the Organization for Economic Cooperation and Development (OECD). In fact, whole nations are being evaluated and ranked by how "efficiently" they spend and educate their children.

Thus, a *ratio* of *inputs*—including funds, staffing, effort, and other resources—can be made to *outputs*, such as: (1) children graduating from schools and colleges; (2) test results when compared with other areas and nations; and (3) school graduate success as measured by income, investment, and quality of life (families, children, income, and lifestyle).

## TERM 3: EQUALITY

Perhaps the most basic notion and effort in American education has long been *equality* under the U.S. Constitution—and state and local laws and policies—that sought to eliminate such "inequalities" as slavery, racial school segregation, and discrimination against poor and/or disabled, and non-English-speaking children. Equality questions whether public education is truly available, similar, and working for all children, regardless of ability wealth, and/or location.

In the past seventy-five years, the United States has worked hard to *equalize* school enrollment and access by eliminating racial segregation, enforced by the courts and important cases like the earliest one in Kansas, the *Brown v. Board of Education* case. As Darling-Hammond (2012) stated years ago in a speech:

> Many people are asking: Why are we here? We are here because we are committed to a strong public education system that works for ALL our children. We

are here because we want to prepare children for the 21st century world they are entering, not for an endless series of multiple-choice tests that increasingly deflect us from our mission to teach them well. We are here to protest the policies that produce the increasingly segregated and underfunded schools so many of our children attend, and we are here to represent the parents, educators and community members who fight for educational opportunity for them against the odds every day. (p. 2)

## TERM 4: EQUITY

Besides being a complex concept, *equity* is perhaps the most important, as it qualifies as a crucial *moral* concern. For example, what is "right" or "wrong" about the levels of school funding, and what can the authorities do to correct it? Ultimately, *equity* means *"fairness"* for those children and their families (and communities and societies) affected by it? The concept can be seen as local, regional, racial, socio-economic, and even nationally and internationally, depending on what analysis units or students groups—and where—are being compared.

For example, school segregation, discrimination against poor students, and/or disabled children—and other special needs kids—are all examples of what societies often face in education and work to combat. Thus, the United States has sought in the past fifty years to do the following: (1) end racial segregation; (2) serve children in poor neighborhoods; and (3) help children with intellectual, linguistic, emotional, and physical problems or disabilities. As Einhorn explained:

> We are here to say it is not acceptable for the wealthiest country in the world to be cutting millions of dollars from schools serving our neediest students; to be cutting teachers by the tens of thousands, to be eliminating art, music, PE, counselors, nurses, librarians, and libraries (where they weren't already gone, as in California); to be increasing class sizes to 40 or 50 in Los Angeles and Detroit, come out on top. (Einhorn, 2007, p. 121)

## REFERENCES

Cooper, B. S., & Gargan, A. (2009). Rubrics in education: Old term, new meanings. *Phi Delta Kappan, 91*(1), pp. 54–55.

Darling-Hammond, L. (July 4, 2012). 2012 UNESCO Summit—A talk by Linda Darling-Hammond. Summit Review, pp. 23–30.

Eichhorn, J. W. (September 2007). *How the world's best-performing school systems come out on top.* New York, NY: McKinsey & Co.

McTighe, J., & O'Connor, K. (2005). Seven practices for effective teaching. *Educational Leadership, 63*(3), pp. 10–17.

Molinar, M. (September 3, 2014). "U.S. 'education efficiency' ranks in bottom 50 percent, study says," *Market Brief K-12. Education Week*, p. 1.

Scheerens, J. (2013). *What is effective schooling? A review of current thought and practice*. International Baccalaureate Organization. Twente, the Netherlands: University of Twente Press.

Shute, J., & Cooper, B. S. (2015). *Fixing truancy now: Inviting students back to class*. Lanham, MD: Rowman & Littlefield.

# Section II

# FINANCIAL MANAGEMENT PROCESSES

This section of the book provides the methods, skills, and tools for raising, allocating, and evaluating the use of funds for principals and staff at the school site—thus, school leaders use their funds effectively as part of the school operations and management.

## Chapter 2

# "N.A.P.E.R." Steps in a Budget Model and Process

## Stephen Coffin and Bruce S. Cooper

### INTRODUCTION

School principals are critical leaders in finding, organizing, and using education resources in their schools to meet the various needs of their students and staff. Budgeting—as a process—is critical in almost every effort; and learning to budget—the process and the products—is also all-important. This chapter presents a tried-and-true process for successful, adaptive budgeting for programs in schools. We have crafted a five-step process, called N.A.P.E.R., to make this happen; and we show how, when, and why. First, let us define the five-step process:

### First, "N"—NEEDS:

Develop and explain all *needs* by asking the stakeholders what they want and require to improve their program or classrooms and then compile needs without any specific order. Making sure that all stakeholders are represented is central to developing a consensus and support for the effort. Districts increasingly are involving teachers in the process. School Business Administrators should ask principals to question supervisors or departmental heads, then, to ask their teachers what they believe their educational needs are.

Teachers should identify needs such as classroom furniture, ceiling, window, heating, electrical, water if applicable, supplies, materials, computers or computer time, whiteboards, books, paper goods, manipulative items; and other classroom items, but not salary or benefit items which are controlled centrally.

### Second "A"—ASSUMPTIONS:

Have each stakeholder and budget person develop an undergirding set of *assumptions and arguments* for each item in the proposed budget. Providing assumptions to support each identified need is essential. Assumptions address the "why is this needed?" question and help in decision-making. Stakeholders must keep in mind that their assumptions may not be and are not always obvious to those who will use their input to make final budgetary decisions. Assumptions help to support the level of need and justify the costs and efforts.

### Third "P"—PRIORITIES:

Prioritize all *needs*, based on their assumptions and implied importance. Teachers should and can prioritize their needs before submitting them to their supervisors or department heads—which in turn would lead to their particular needs, assumptions, prioritization, and rationale before submitting them to their principal. In turn, the principal adds his or her needs, assumptions, prioritization, and rationale to the document including his or her overview of his or her school's needs, assumptions, prioritization, and rationale.

### Fourth "E"—EXPENDITURES:

How to organize to make it happen, based on finance availability and expenditures? Without adequate funding, the program will have difficulty operating and growing. How to get organized and staffed in schools to make the budget work and real, and effective?

### Fifth: Double-"R"—RATIONALE and REVIEW:

And finally, how to provide a RATIONALE and REVIEW PROCESS for each priority, per item, will help justify and improve its relative importance in the budget, and how the program or other budget uses may be reviewed and evaluated at some point. Each level of the process should provide a rationale, starting with the teachers. (N.A.P.E.R.R. should be truly based on teachers' inputs and school and classroom collective needs.)

Once N.A.P.E.R. is completed—with all stakeholders active in the process—the leaders must see if anyone receives cuts to aid or meet sudden increased costs. If this results in a budget gap, teachers and school building leaders can quickly contact each provider of that item, reassess its priority, and make selective rather applying across-the-board percentage cuts (unsound and usually backfire).

Projected program and service offerings can and often do change during the process, making budgeting a dynamic process; however, at a certain point having done the best possible effort, the budget is submitted for board of education's (BOE's) approval or central office's approval if a private or charter school, which often includes board of governors/trustees' approval.

N.A.P.E.R. can be used in schools to help develop budgets, large or small, within departments, schools, or districts in both the public and private sectors. Students and others have successfully used N.A.P.E.R. in job interviews and in their careers. N.A.P.E.R. provides a sound conceptual and practical framework for budgeting.

The step in developing a budget for a school is to determine the needs. Edwards et al. (2000) explain that budget determination is a two-step process, as follows:

> First to satisfy their statutory duties LEAs supervised the introduction of internal systems of budgetary control and school development planning in schools. Thus, control procedures were largely designed by internal auditors, who sought to provide an audit trail and to ensure financial probity mainly to satisfy external legitimacy, rather than to influence internal decision-making.
>
> Second, the specific nature of the relationship between budgeting and strategy varies between schools, as the extent of formalized planning differs; but in general there is a very loose coupling between strategic objectives and budget expenditures. (pp. 1–2)

Finally, since most—if not all—schools have needs, the step is to set priorities, share them, and make a case for funding and meeting the needs. N.A.P.E.R. allows leaders to follow sound steps in setting and gaining the funds, at the school and classroom levels, to make the goals work.

## REFERENCE

Edwards, P., Ezzamel, M., McLean, C., & Robson, K. (2000). Budgeting and strategy in schools: The elusive link. *Financial Accountability & Management, 16*(4), pp. 21–36.

## Chapter 3

# Strategic Budgeting for School Principals

### Lawrence O. Picus

When asked about their discretionary dollars available for use at their school, principals often answer that they have very limited amounts of money to use outside of prescribed district and state requirements, sometimes citing a number as low as $10,000 or $15,000 in a school with as many as 400 or 500 students. This figure seems artificially low and suggests that principals wanting to make significant changes in the strategic management of their school to improve student performance have few options.

This chapter argues that school principals have much more discretion in the allocation and use of resources than they often think are available; and the chapter suggests that the first step in thinking about how to allocate resources is to focus on the personnel whom they can employ and not only on the so-called discretionary dollars available at their school. School leadership requires principals to use the *personnel resources* at their disposal to employ staff that research shows will improve student learning.

This chapter explains that the role of the principal in developing a school's budget goes far beyond finding a way to balance flows of dollars to the school with expenditures and that successful principals identify ways to use all their staff resources to implement strategies and programs focused on the learning needs of the students in their school. Ensuring that the resources and expenditures of a school are always balanced is part of this task.

However, in most school districts, numbers of school site personnel are assigned by the district using formulas based on the numbers and characteristics of students (e.g., Hartman, 1988). How those personnel resources are utilized to engage and support students is critical to improving student learning. Yet many principals do not consider the alternative ways personnel can be allocated to implement research-based strategies that can improve student outcomes.

Allocating personnel resources for high student performance requires strong leadership skills to establish a "theory of action" about how to organize the school for learning, as well as the ability to identify, recruit, and retain teachers and other school personnel who can successfully implement the school's strategic plans. These tasks are much more complex than the traditional notion of balancing the marginal dollars available to a school.

The rest of this chapter discusses the importance of a strategic plan for leading a school, as well as how personnel resources can be reallocated to implement that plan, and the barriers school leaders need to overcome as they implement their plan. It starts, however, with a short discussion of overall school resources and the implications of variation across states and school districts.

## AVAILABILITY OF SCHOOL RESOURCES

According to the U.S. Census Bureau (2016), in fiscal year (FY) 2013–2014, public K-12 school systems spent a total of $613.6 billion, of which $546.7 billion (89.1 percent) was for current expenses—which included the resources over which a school principal is likely to have some responsibility. This amounted to an average of $11,009 per pupil, but ranged from a low of $6,500 per pupil in Utah to over $20,000 per pupil in New York. These substantial differences clearly have an impact on the resources available to school principals. This is most clearly shown in data pertaining to pupil-to-teacher ratios, which ranged from 10.6 students per teacher in Vermont to 24.3 pupils per teacher in California in the fall of 2013 (Snyder, de Brey, and Dillow, 2016). Notably, the pupil-to-teacher ratio in the highest and lowest spending states is 23.0 to 1 in Utah and 13.2 in New York.

If one looks more closely at the New York and Utah data, New York spends +3.17 times more per pupil than Utah, but the pupil-to-/teacher ratio in Utah is only 1.74 times larger than that in New York, suggesting that there is not a straightforward one-to-one relationship between per-pupil spending levels and resulting class size. This is likely a result of higher average 2013–2014 teacher salaries in New York ($78,835) compared to Utah ($52,806).

While New York average salaries were the highest in the nation in 2013–2014, Utah salaries were just over $10,000 higher than the lowest average salary in South Dakota of $41,649 (NEA, 2016). These comparisons are complicated by the fact that the National Center for Education Statistics (NCES) definition of "teachers" is broader than classroom instructors, and includes a range of other school-based personnel. Moreover, it is likely that individual states, and even districts, compute the number of teachers somewhat differently leading to variation in what is and is not included in the NCES data.

Although it is unlikely that completely consistent definitions of even basic terms like "teacher" can ever be developed for comparative use in a diverse federal system like the United States with fifty states and over 14,000 school districts, the variation found lends support to the idea of developing initial budgets at the school site on the basis of personnel positions. Districts allocate positions to schools with varying levels of control, frequently leaving the final assignment to the principal.

Equally important to successful school leadership is how personnel (and overall school) time is used. Principals often have considerable control over how time is allocated within minimum time requirements established by states, districts, and/or teacher contracts.

Depending on state and local policy and local teacher contract agreements, principals also have control over average class sizes in many schools, providing the ability to consider alternative personnel allocation strategies. How a principal chooses to use the personnel at his or her school is the focus of the next section of this chapter.

## ORGANIZING A SCHOOL FOR HIGH PERFORMANCE

The first step in developing a budget focused on student performance is to create a strategic plan for allocating resources within a school. That is, how are the personnel and associated materials and supplies used at the school? This includes such basic calculations as average class size, number of core and elective teachers, and teacher and student support personnel, including instructional coaches, counselors, librarians, teaching aides, and teacher tutors. A school typically is assigned a number of certificated staff based on the number and characteristics of the students at that school.

How those positions are used is often something that can be decided at the school level, although many principals are reluctant to change personnel use patterns that already exist. Deciding how to allocate these positions provides a principal with the single greatest ability to change the way school resources are used to improve student learning; thus, having a theory of action or model of resource allocation is essential to strategic budget management at the school level.

Allocation of human resources at the school includes consideration of average class size, number of core subjects (language arts, math, science, social studies, and world languages) and electives, allocation of staff for coaching, counseling, pupil support, help for struggling students, and providing planning and collaboration time for teachers. Structuring the school day to meet the needs of all students is an important part of that process as well.

## The Evidence-Based Model

While principals can implement different strategies, this chapter focuses on Odden's and Picus's evidence-based (EB) model (see Odden and Picus, 2014) as a good working example. The Evidence-Based (EB) model relies on existing educational research to identify the resources needed to ensure that all students in a school have a sufficient opportunity to meet their state's performance standards. The EB model has been used in several states to identify adequate levels of resources to fund schools and is used as the basis for the school finance funding formula in Wyoming and Arkansas. It has been used in many more states to estimate adequate funding levels. A full description of the EB model is available in Odden and Picus (2014), and at www.picusod den.com.

The EB model estimates school resources at the elementary, intermediate, and high school levels, relying on a prototypical school model for each. Table 3.1 summarizes the types of resources included in the EB model. The table includes resources for the central office to be comprehensive, but a principal needs to focus most on the first three panels of the table—staff resources, resources for struggling students, and dollar per pupil resources. The order of display is intentional, as it displays the major resource needs of a school in order of the total share of the budget each of the three categories includes. That is expenditures for staff resources for core programs likely represent the largest share of a school's budget, and the dollar per pupil dollar is likely the smallest share.[1] On average, the non-centrally office functions are likely to include between 80 and 85 percent of a school district's budget, making the role of a principal in allocating school resources for student performance critical to success.

Staff positions are then allocated to a school site, based on the enrollment of the school. For example, teachers in grades PK–3 are resourced at one teacher per fifteen students and for grades 4–12 at one teacher per twenty-five students. Additional elective teachers are provided at the rate of 20 percent of the core teachers for elementary and intermediate schools and 33 percent for high schools.

These elective teachers provide time for elementary school teachers to have planning periods and to establish blocks of time each week for teachers to collaborate. At the high school level (and in departmentalized intermediate schools), elective teachers provide resources to ensure that class sizes are approximately twenty-five when students take, for example, six classes a day and teachers teach five classes a day.

A figure of 33 percent for high school elective teachers is used to enable block schedules—where classes meet for two consecutive periods every other day—and allow teachers to have a full block for planning each day. Resources

**Table 3.1. Evidence Based Model School Resources**

Staff resources for core programs
Core teachers (pre-kindergarten [PK] through high school)
Elective teachers
Instructional coaches
Core tutors (provided one-to-one or small group instruction for struggling students)
Substitute teachers
Core guidance counselors
Nurses
Supervisory aides
Library media specialists
Principals and assistant principals
School site secretarial staff
Resources for struggling students (based on numbers of low-income and English-language learner [ELL] students)
Tutors (provided one-to-one or small group instruction for struggling students)
Additional pupil support (counselors, social workers, etc.)
Extended day programs
Summer school programs
ELL programs
Alternative schools
Special education
Dollar per student resources
Gifted and talented
Professional development
Instructional materials
Assessments
Technology
Career and technical education equipment
Extra duty funds and student activities
Central office functions
Maintenance and operations
Central office staffing

are available to a school for professional development (instructional coaches, additional pay for additional professional development (PD) days for teachers, and funds to hire consultants to work with teachers and schools).

Teachers, tutors, and counselors are provided to help struggling students and to offer academic advisement as part of the core resources of a school. In addition to the core resources, additional staff is provided to a school based on the number of low-income and ELL students enrolled at the school. The assumption is that the greater the number of low-income and ELL students in a school, the greater likelihood that higher percentages of students will require additional tutoring and support services, so additional personnel resources are provided as the number of these students increases.

## Why Allocating Personnel Resources Matters

Because the evidence-based model relies on extant research it continues to evolve and change over time. A review of the many individual state adequacy studies, available at www.picusodden.com, shows that the model has been adapted for the specific circumstances of each of the states where it has been used. While the overall allocation of personnel resources in each state EB model is generally the same, the total costs of the model across states vary substantially.

This cost is a function of personnel cost differences across the states. As shown above, the average teacher salary in South Dakota is only 58.2 percent of the average teacher salary in New York, a difference of over $37,000 a year. When total personnel costs are computed (salaries plus benefits), this disparity grows as many benefits are funded based on a percentage of salaries.

Assuming the elements of the EB model were identical in the two states, elementary schools with the same enrollment and same percentages of low-income and ELL students would generate, on average, barely more than half of the dollars a similar elementary school in New York would generate.

This is important for a principal to realize as he or she organizes a school for high achievement. There are vastly different choices a principal can make depending on the state where he or she is located. Although South Dakota is a low-spending state ($8,881 per pupil in 2013–2014), it has a relatively low pupil-to-teacher ratio as well (13.8) because of the low teacher salaries.

California, on the other hand, has among the highest average teacher salary of $71,396, but relatively low per-pupil spending of $9,595, resulting in a pupil-to-teacher ratio of 24.3. If an elementary school principal in California wanted to have average class sizes of fifteen (grades PK–3) and twenty-five (grades 4–5), he or she would have a much harder time finding the resources to hire enough teachers than would a principal in either New York, with high spending and high salaries, or South Dakota, with low spending and low salaries. As described in the next section, these realities constrain principals in different ways.

## STRATEGIC BUDGETING DECISIONS

The previous section suggested that dollars per pupil alone do not drive the resources available to provide educational programs at a school. As that section suggested, the problem is more complex and the available staffing is in part a function of both spending and salary levels. As a result, once a principal has identified how he or she wants to staff the school, a number of strategic resource allocation decisions need to be made. Once the staffing pattern the school can put in place has been determined the principal then needs to identify, hire, train, and retain the staff to implement the plan.

The focus of this section, and this chapter generally, is how to identify the desired personnel resources and what trade-offs need to be made if the total number of desired personnel exceeds available resources. These constraints include legal requirements, state and district policies, contract obligations, and local customs or practices. Each of these is discussed following a discussion of establishing personnel allocations within a school.

## Deciding How to Allocate (or Reallocate) Personnel Resources at the School Level

In previous work, in states that have used the EB model to allocate school funding, we have observed how districts and schools elect to use the resources available to produce student achievement. In both Arkansas and Wyoming, where we have the most experience to date, we found that allocating personnel to the functions described in the EB model takes time, even if that is a school's eventual goal.

In 2006 we found very few changes in the way resources were allocated by schools in Arkansas despite the infusion of substantial new fiscal resources identified through an EB model (Odden, Picus, and Goetz, 2006). By 2014, when we were asked to help recalibrate the Arkansas's funding formula, we noted that more districts and schools were using their personnel in ways more closely associated with the patterns established by the EB model (Odden, Picus, and Price, 2014).

Similarly, in Wyoming, our initial field studies of all the schools in the state suggested little initial change in the allocation and use of resources, although in recent professional development meetings with school personnel, we have heard considerably more descriptions that suggest the EB model is the basis for resource allocation decisions (Picus, et al. 2008; Odden and Picus, 2015).

How a principal changes the allocation of personnel resources is critical to his or her success in improving student learning. Often at first blush, when the core teacher resources generated for a school are estimated, it seems that the model provides fewer resources than what already exist at the school. But when all the additional personnel included in the EB model are included, the total number of certificated staff in a given school more closely parallels that school's reality. What is often the case is that there is roughly the same number of certificated staff in the school, they are just doing something different. In cases where resources are not adequate to meet the EB model's recommendations, principals need to prioritize how they want to allocate their staff. This entails trade-offs between smaller class sizes and the employment of instructional coaches and other personnel who provide services to students.

Substantial evidence shows that employment of instructional coaching, for example, is likely to be more cost-effective than further reductions in class size, particularly since the addition of one position to a school has a marginal, at best, impact on average class size if used as a core teacher, but could have a much larger impact as a coach. But what if the principal does not have resources for an additional staff member but wants to employ a coach from within his or her existing staff? The first option might be to reassign a staff member who does not have a regular classroom assignment, for example, a counselor or other student services position. If this is not possible, the principal may consider an increase in average class size to fill a coaching position. Table 3.2 shows the trade-offs a principal might face when trying to estimate the impact of such a decision.

Table 3.2 assumes a school of 400 students and 20 core teachers. As the first row of the table shows, if there are no coaches, all twenty core teachers can be assigned to a classroom with an average class size of twenty. If the school wanted to assign one teacher to be a coach, there were be nineteen remaining teachers and an average class size of 21.05 students. Similarly, if the school wanted two coaches, say for example, a reading coach and a math coach, then the remaining eighteen teachers would have an average of 22.22 students per class.

The trade-off is clear, and the remaining question is to what extent does the school's leadership think employment of one or two coaches will help improve student performance, given the average class size will increase by one student per teacher? While it is unlikely a school with 400 students would need more than two coaches, table 3.2 shows the impact as more teachers are utilized as coaches.

Making similar trade-offs is more complicated when average class sizes are larger, or when restrictions make it harder to shift roles and responsibilities, but it is still possible over time. For example, federal funding restrictions

**Table 3.2.    Impact of Additional Coaches on Average Class Size: School of 400 Students**

| No. of Coaches | Number of Teachers | Average Class Size |
|:--------------:|:------------------:|:------------------:|
| 0 | 20 | 20.00 |
| 1 | 19 | 21.05 |
| 2 | 18 | 22.22 |
| 3 | 17 | 23.53 |
| 4 | 16 | 25.00 |
| 5 | 15 | 26.67 |

often make it impossible for a school to use a Title 1 funded position to serve as a tutor for all students. But it may be possible to utilize that federally funded position for several federal program needs, thus freeing up a teaching position that does not have restricted funding to meet the specific needs of a school's students.

The key is identifying all the needs of the student population, and then finding the resources necessary to meet them. Often through reassignment of personnel or the combination of responsibilities in different patterns than what exist at present, additional student needs can be met with the same number of credentialed positions. Similarly, how time is used in the school can also enable a school to enact programs that lead to improved student learning.

## Alternative Uses of Time

There are also several research-based practices that can help improve student outcomes with little or no cost. Evidence about the importance of teacher collaboration (in addition to individual planning time) suggests that organizing school time so that teachers have time to work together in same grade and same subject teams leads to improved curriculum, better teaching, and often a stronger school program (see, e.g., DuFour and DuFour, 2012). Strategies that provide for more collaboration and planning time require greater attention to the organization of the overall school day and the use of elective teachers to ensure that all core teachers have access to these planning and collaborative resources.

Often school norms or contract requirements make identification of additional time for collaboration difficult, but over time and with the careful analysis of the terms of a district's contract with its teachers, it is often possible to find additional time resources.

For example, one district had a requirement that any time the district required for teacher work outside of the classroom it had to be accompanied by the same amount of additional individual planning time, effectively doubling the time requirements of identifying a fifteen-minute block each day. By lengthening recess to fifteen minutes (from ten) the teaching contract allowed that time to be considered as planning time rather than "free" time, effectively finding the fifteen minutes a day of individual planning needed for part of the collaborative time the district sought. Similar shifts and adjustments to school schedules can often yield similar results.

At the high school level, a block schedule can also provide more time if a school is adequately staffed to provide a full daily block of planning time for teachers. Under that arrangement, a teacher has the equivalent of two periods a day (in one block) to use for planning and collaboration. Schools with a seven period day where teachers teach five classes can also arrange for this, although doing so either requires more elective teachers to ensure that classes remain at twenty-five or larger classes.

The so-called seven and five classes scheduled also frequently shorten the length of each class period, thereby reducing class time. If the seventh class is another elective, there is no sustentative evidence the extra class (compared to more time in class with a six-period day) will lead to improved student performance.

## BARRIERS TO REALLOCATION OF RESOURCES

Many of the ideas presented above seem straightforward, yet school principals often have trouble trying to implement them. State laws and policies often make changes difficult or impossible. Many states have maximum class size requirements for some elementary grades, or even for certain subject classes at the high school level. Some limit the number of students a teacher can have in classes during the day. Vermont, for example, limits the number of students a teacher can face to 100 per day, effectively limiting high school class sizes to an average of twenty students.

Other state laws provide protections for teachers that make transfers or removal harder, and other states have minimum number of days and contact minutes for students that must be met. Many states offer waivers for some state requirements, and in some instances school district requirements can be adjusted as well.

Other challenges that principals may face include the use of restricted funds. Many compensatory educational programs such as the Federal Government's Title 1 program and various programs to serve ELL students come with strict requirements regarding how the funds can be used. State programs for compensatory education and ELL students often come with funding restrictions as well. It is incumbent on a good principal leader to identify ways the money can be spent appropriately and legally and at the same time meet the needs of the students in his or her school. Creative personnel allocation decisions can help use these important, but restricted, funding sources effectively.

School district contracts with teacher organizations can also limit the flexibility a principal has in allocating and using school personnel. Contracts often limit class size or the number of minutes a teacher can teach daily. They may also control how planning and/or collaborative time can be allocated and used. In situations where contract limitations exist, school leaders need to work with the teachers at the school and together identify creative ways to establish programs that meet the strategic plans of the school.

Establishing work schedules and class times so that more collaborative time is available—and holding faculty meetings after school hours may be possible—helps with the time, but it is up to the school personnel to work within the contract's framework as well as the goals of the school's plan. If school plans are agreed to by all or most of the teachers, waivers to contract provisions may be available. The key is finding a way to work together to resolve contract issues at the school site, regardless of the bargaining climate at the district—if possible.

## CONCLUSION

This discussion has focused on alternative budgeting strategies for school site leaders. The focus has been heavily on the allocation and use of personnel resources rather than on a discussion of how to balance the dollars and cents of a school site's budget. The reason for this is grounded in the argument that how personnel are used at a school will have the largest impact on student learning and achievement and thus should receive the most attention.

Despite the differences in teacher pay—salary schedules often have a range of two-to-one from the lowest block of the salary matrix to the highest—most schools are essentially funded at the district's average compensation cost per teacher. That is, a district determines how many teacher positions it can afford, and then determines how many positions are available at each school.

The cost of an individual teacher (salary and benefits) is not a direct concern to most school principals in almost all school districts in the United States.

This "average cost" funding makes it possible for a principal to seek out the teachers that most closely meet his or her vision for the education program of the school. It does this by enabling the principal to "invest" in the future of that teacher through strong professional development so they will be able to retain the teacher without worrying about increasing costs of paying that teacher's salary and benefits. Focusing on teachers who are the right "fit" for an individual school is the first step in developing a strong, focused educational program aimed at the needs of that school's students.

Another challenge in implementing strategic budget changes is the time frame. In education, we are used to the coming and going of educational fads. A strategic plan lays out the intended organization and goals of a school and then works hard every year to implement that plan. This means that it may not be possible to fund all the details of the plan in the first year or two. Consequently, the principal must work to slowly build toward the planed resource allocations, focusing initially on the most cost-effective strategies, and implementing those that are important, but less cost-effective further down the road.

In the end, all resources can be translated into dollar resources, and all budgets must be in balance; so a final step is to ensure that the cost of personnel and other resources does not exceed the available resources from year to year. This often leads to the need to make hard choices about which resources should be maintained at current levels, which should be increased and which should be decreased. Knowing the most cost-effective way to allocate resources to improve student learning is an essential skill for any school principal today.

## NOTE

1. This could vary as a school with a small percentage of low-income and ELL students may generate fewer resources for struggling students than it does through the dollar per pupil resources.

## REFERENCES

DuFour, R., & DuFour, R. (2012). *The school leader's guide to professional learning communities at work (essentials for principals)*. Indianapolis, IN: Solution Tree.

Hartman, William T. (1988). *School district budgeting*. Englewood Cliffs, NJ: Prentice Hall.

NEA. (2016). *Rankings & estimates*. Washington, DC: National Education Association. Available at https://www.nea.org/assets/docs/2016_ NEA_Rankings_And_ Estimates. pdf.

Odden, A., & Picus, L. O. (2015). *2015 Wyoming recalibration report*. Prepared for the Wyoming Select Committee on School Finance Recalibration. North Hollywood, CA: Lawrence O. Picus and Associates. Available at http://picusodden.com/wp-content/uploads/2013/09/Picus-Odden-Nov-2015-WY-Recalib-Report.pdf.

Odden, A., Picus, L. O., & Goetz, M. (2006). *Recalibrating the Arkansas School Funding Structure: Final report submitted to the Adequacy Study Oversight Sub-Committee of the House and Senate Interim Committees on Education of the Arkansas General Assembly*. North Hollywood, CA: Lawrence O. Picus and Associates. Available at http://picusodden.com/wp-content/uploads/2013/09/AR-Recalibration-Report-August-30-2006.pdf.

Odden, A., Picus, L. O., & Price, S. (2014). *Desk audit of the Arkansas School Funding Matrix and developing an understanding of the potential costs of broadband access for all schools*. Prepared for the Arkansas House and Senate Committees on Education. North Hollywood, CA: Lawrence O. Picus and Associates. Available at http://picusodden.com/wp-content/uploads/2014/09/9-5-2014-Picus-Odden-Asso.-AR-Desk-Audit-9-5-14a.pdf.

Odden, A. R., & Picus, L. O. (2014). *School finance: A policy perspective* (5th ed.). New York: McGraw-Hill.

Picus, L. O., Odden, A., Aportela, A., Mangan, M. T., & Goetz, M. (2008). *Implementing school finance adequacy: School level resource use in Wyoming following adequacy-oriented finance reform.* Prepared for the Wyoming Legislative Service Office. North Hollywood, CA: Lawrence O. Picus and Associates. Available at http://legisweb.state.wy.us/2008/interim/schoolfinance/Resources.pdf.

Snyder, T. D., de Brey, D., & Dillow, S. A. (2016). *Digest of Education Statistics: 2015.* National Center for Education Statistics, Institute of Education Sciences. U.S. Department of Education: Washington DC. (NCES 2016–014). Available at http://nces.ed.gov/pubs2016/2016014.pdf.

U.S. Census Bureau. (2016). *Public education finances: 2014.* G14-ASPEF. Washington, DC: U.S. Government Printing Office. Available at https://census.gov/content/dam/Census/library/publications/2016/econ/g14-aspef.pdf.

*Chapter 4*

# Enrollment Projections

*Students Drive the "Budget Bus"*

William Hartman and Robert Schoch

Projections of student enrollments provide the baseline estimates of the level of district operations *and expenditures* for the upcoming year. As such, they represent the initial step in preparing the district's budget. Accurate projections are essential since they determine or influence many of financial estimates that go into the budget, particularly in the instructional area. Figure 4.1 illustrates the major connections that link student projections to district operations and budget estimates; practically all of the important areas of school- and district-level activities are included.

## LINKAGES BETWEEN STUDENT ENROLLMENTS AND BUDGETS

- **Personnel.** Accurate student enrollment projections are critical for the personnel components of the budget since salaries and benefits costs—for district staff demands, based on enrollment—represent the largest expenditure areas in a school district. On one hand, getting the appropriate number of staff to meet the educational needs of students is vital to providing an effective education. On the other hand, the educational needs must be balanced with the fiscal constraints the district faces.

Most types of personnel requirements are derived directly or indirectly from estimates of the number of students to be served. Establishing the suitable number of various types of personnel is generally driven by student enrollment projections at different grade levels and for different student classes, courses, and needs. For teachers and instructional support personnel, districts often have board-established policies for acceptable student-to-staff ratios.

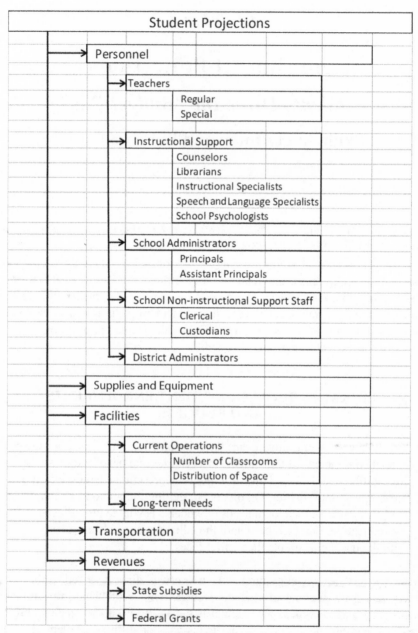

Figure 4.1.   Enrollment Influences on Budget Areas

For example, the number of teachers required is frequently determined using the estimated enrollments and district student/teacher policies. Similar determinations are made for other professional instructional personnel and district policies concerning expected caseloads.

- **Non-personnel Items.** Allocations to schools for instructional books and supplies, materials, and equipment are frequently made on a dollar-per-student basis. Coupled with the projected student enrollments, this provides a pool of money to the school that can be used by the principal and teachers to provide these instructional resources.
- **Transportation.** The number of buses and driver/maintenance staff required are affected by student enrollments and bussing routes and distances. Minimizing the number of buses—subject to student safety, quality of service, and district policies—has important budgetary implications. For example, the distribution of students among elementary, middle, and high schools—and the location of those schools—affect bus transportation routes; location of students, combined with district policies on walk-to-school distances, will determine those students eligible for transportation services; ride time limitations, particularly in sparsely populated areas, may lead to more inefficient and costly operations. The number of students attending schools outside their attendance zone to attend specialized placements also affects transportation needs. In some states, public schools must also transport resident students attending private or charter schools outside district boundaries.
- **Revenues.** On the revenue side, budget estimates of certain revenue sources may also be directly related to the number of students, *with varying needs*, in the school district and each school. Specific state subsidies and/or federal aid, which are distributed to districts on a dollar-per-student basis, are determined by multiplying the number of students by the dollar-per-student aid amount. In some cases, these subsidies may be based on the number of certain categories of students, such as poverty status or disability. This will require district enrollment estimates of these subgroups of students for budgeting projected revenues.
- **Facilities.** The needs for facilities, such as number of schools and/or classrooms and other rooms, both current and long term, are calculated using the projected student enrollments. Estimations of schools and other district instructional and administrative facilities are long-term decisions. Figure 4.2 below provides an illustration of this procedure along with several enrollment-to-budget instances from other areas that are driven by projected enrollments.

As an illustration, if an elementary school was projected to have 500 students for the upcoming year, district administrators could then apply the

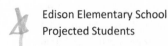

| Edison Elementary School | | Current | in Five Years |
|---|---|---|---|
| Projected Students | | 500 | 400 |

| Budget Item | Student-to-Staff Ratio | Staff Required | Staff Required |
|---|---|---|---|
| Classroom Teacher | 20 | 25 | 20 |
| Math Specialist | 200 | 2.5 | 2 |
| Speech and Language Specialist | 250 | 2 | 1.6 |
| Classrooms | 20 | 25 | 20 |
| Instructional Supplies | dollar per Student | | |
| Equipment | $75 | $37,500 | $30,000 |
| | $50 | $25,000 | $20,000 |
| State General Education Subsidy | $5,000 | $2,500,000 | $2,000,000 |
| (Note: The dollar per student amount would be applied to all student in the district not just those in this school to estimate district revenues from the state.) | | | |

**Figure 4.2.   Examples of Enrollments to Budget Items**

district's student-to-staff ratios to estimate the amount/numbers of staff and facility requirements needed for the upcoming year. In the example, with a maximum capacity of twenty-five students per classroom, the school of 500 students would need a minimum of about twenty-five classroom teachers to serve its students' classrooms.

Practically, this would mean implementing the policy using an average classroom size for the school with some classrooms having slightly more or fewer students than the policy specifies due to actual numbers of students per grade. Instructional specialists often have assigned caseloads of students and can serve students in multiple schools. Given the district's staffing policy for math specialists of a caseload of 200 students, the district would assign 2.5 math specialists to the school. Likely the 0.5 specialist in Edison Elementary would also be assigned to another school for the other 0.5 full-time equivalent (FTE) for the position.

If all teachers had their own classroom, the school would have to have twenty-five classrooms to house its students. The students will also gener-ate monies for instructional supplies and equipment for use by teachers in their classrooms. District policies often establish an amount per student to be provided to schools through their budget. In this example, with an allocation of $75 per student for supplies, the school would receive $37,500 to provide these instructional items for 500 students in the school.

Transportation is a budget item that is also tied to the number of students to be served, along with (1) where they live and distance from home to school, and back; (2) what schools they attend; and (3) a variety of district policies regarding their transportation. All of these variables combine into a bus schedule and routing plan to determine the number of buses that will be needed to provide the necessary services to the kids. At an annual operating cost of $50,000 to $100,000 per bus, these services—whether provided by the district or contacted to a bus company vendor—are expensive and are derived from student enrollment projections and geographical district layout.

## CONTEXT FOR MAKING STUDENT ENROLLMENT PROJECTIONS

**Counting Students.** Several different approaches can be used in counting the number of students in a school district. The approach selected will probably be determined by state department of education's student-accounting definitions. The two principal approaches for measuring the number of students are average daily membership (ADM) and average daily attendance (ADA). ADM counts all students enrolled in school (i.e., on the membership list) whether or not they are actually attending school at the time the student count is taken. ADA, by contrast, counts only those students actually attending school at the time the count is made.

The difference between the two approaches is how they treat absences; ADM counts include absent students when the enrollment is determined, while ADA counts exclude absences, counting only those students physically present at the time the enrollment is determined. As a result, ADM counts will always be higher than ADA counts, a situation that disadvantages school districts with high absentee rates. With the higher count, budgets based on ADM plans for the full complement of students served by the school or district and provides a cushion in terms of instructional staff and resources and classroom space for days where a higher number of students may be in attendance. Modifications to the basic approaches are possible—including excused absences as part of ADA counts, for example.

Another differentiation that may be made in student counts is enrollments versus FTE counts. Enrollment generally corresponds to head counts of students, where every student enrolled in a program counts as one student, whether full time or part time. FTE counts adjust the number of students reported to only include the actual amount of time in a program. A student who participates part time in a particular program is counted only for that fraction of time in that program. For example, in a student accounting system utilizing FTE counts, a student with a mild disability—receiving special education in a resource room for one period out of five periods in the school day—would have an FTE count of 0.20 in special education and 0.80 in regular education. This allocates the student count for students by the time they spend in different programs.

ADM counts provide a more appropriate estimate of students for districts to plan and budget for programs; ADA or FTE student counts do not necessarily correspond to the resources and space districts must provide for all students, whether or not they are in attendance on a particular day. The special education student in the previous example will probably require a full complement of services in regular education even though the FTE enrollment is only 0.80.

The period each day spent outside the classroom (e.g., in a resource room setting) is of very little budgetary significance to the regular classroom: the teacher is paid the same, the student's desk remains and takes up the same space, and heat and light consumption are not reduced. Perhaps some instructional materials are not required, but these are usually quite minor. As a result, school districts operating under an ADA or FTE approach may have to maintain two separate, but related student-accounting procedures—one for state reporting and one for local planning and budgeting.

- **Who Does the Projections and When?** Enrollment projections are usually done centrally for the school district, either by district office personnel or through a contract arrangement with an outside consultant. School principals or district department heads can contribute information to the projection process if they have useful knowledge or insights about unusual circumstances that affect the number of students leaving or entering the school in the upcoming year. Projections are generally done early in the school year so that they can be utilized in the district budget process. Often the process will begin in August or September with data gathering by the business office.
- **What Information Is Needed?** The central office personnel responsible for developing projections will collect internal information maintained by the district, such as the latest up-to-date enrollment numbers in the district and in each school, demographic characteristics of current students, and numbers and location of special needs students. Additional external information from the community that will influence the number of students should be gathered during this time as well; possible items would include new or expanding housing developments, planned or announced major

private sector company changes such as new business opening or expanding in the district, or plant or other businesses closing or relocating outside of the district. The impacts of economic activity in the community on future enrollments, both positive and negative, should also be incorporated into the enrollment projection process.

Another important aspect for student enrollment projections is the general student population trends in the district and state. A historical review of five or more past years of enrollment trends can provide important insight into potential future changes. Some questions to ask are: Have the number of students been growing (or steady or declining) in the district in recent years? Are the enrollment trends the same for the elementary level as for the high school level? What have been the birth rates in the district's catchment area? In many ways, districts have a relatively long lead-time to adjust for enrollment changes. Students who will be entering kindergarten next year have already been born five years ago, ample time to plan for staffing and facilities changes.

The upper-level elementary students will progress into high school year after year; again, the numbers and timing of their entry is known well ahead of time. This is not to say that there will be no changes as students advance through the system, or that there will be no migration *into* and/*or* out of the district. However, a relatively reliable baseline estimate of future student enrollments can be determined from past trends and from analyzing potential changes that would alter the past patterns.

• **Types of Students for Projections.** To build the budget for the next FY, *detailed estimates of the number of students to be served in the school district for the upcoming year are needed.* These projections generally are made along several dimensions relevant to educational and budgetary decisions—for example, district total, education level (elementary, middle, high school), school building, grade level, and types of student (regular, exceptional, ELL/limited English proficiency, vocational, and disadvantaged).

These divisions are not mutually exclusive and may overlap within the district—or at a given school to provide greater detail about the students expected for the upcoming year and any particular resource needs that may be required.

Consequently, the categories used by the school district to project next year's student enrollments should correspond to the instructional and instructional support programs the district is planning to provide its students. For example, to meet the curriculum, staffing, and instructional space needs it may be necessary to estimate enrollments of disabled students in multiple dimensions—by exceptionality, by type of instructional and support program, by location, and by service provider (district, contracted special education service organization). This is not to say that every possible permutation of enrollment should be calculated, but that there may be useful sub-projections that focus on student populations of particular interest.

- **Distribution and Use of Projections.** Once the student and staffing projections are completed, the relevant results are provided to the district personnel who are developing the budget requests for each program or organizational area. For example, estimates of individual school enrollments, in total, by grade level, and by relevant demographic groups, are frequently given to building principals to use in their budget preparation activities. Likewise, the special education director would receive estimates of the number of students with disabilities conditions (by type of disability, age, and severity of condition) to establish a baseline for developing a budget request in that area. The enrollment projections would then be used to estimate total personnel requirements and allocation of positions among different grades or types of students, as well as to determine the amount of money available for instructional supplies and equipment.

## ENROLLMENT PROJECTION TECHNIQUES

Several different methods are often used for estimating student enrollments for the upcoming year and beyond. The approaches range from simple to sophisticated, and vary in their reliability. The simplest approach is an "educated guess" by the district superintendent, business manager, and/or others, based on the current enrollments and their projections about what may occur next year. This approach is fast, inexpensive, and understandable. It can also incorporate relevant information about district economic, social, or political conditions into the enrollment estimates. On the other hand, it is also subject to considerable error or bias, since the estimates are often derived from past experience and subjective assessments.

Other more formalized projection approaches have been successful in estimating student enrollments, including various mathematical forecasting techniques for projecting future enrollments based on past trends.[1] However, the basic rationale underlying these extrapolative techniques is the assumption that the same conditions affecting enrollment in the past will continue to prevail in the future. This may not be the case in districts undergoing demographic and economic changes. For example, a district that has been economically depressed and losing population for the past several years may not want to project a decreasing enrollment trend into the next years if several manufacturing firms have opened up new plants in the community—and the economy is showing signs of recovering.

The assumptions and conditions behind enrollment projections should be examined to see if they are still valid in light of what administrators know or believe about the district's condition in the upcoming years. Adjustments can and should be made to the projections calculated by any of the forecasting techniques to reflect accurately the expected changes in the district's future.

**Trend Line Analysis**. Trend line analysis is a form of linear regression that uses the year as the predictor variable and the district enrollment as the dependent, outcome, or predicted variable. With a spreadsheet or a simple statistical program on a computer, it is possible to calculate future enrollments easily. The data needed are the enrollments of the pertinent student populations for each of the past five or six years. Future years' levels are estimated by projecting the trend line from the past years' data and extending it into future years. The statistical methodology of linear regression is used to calculate the line of "best fit" for the previous enrollments. The result is an equation of a straight line. This is represented by the trend line on the chart in figure 4.3.

Using the past five years' enrollments, a trend line is shown and the past five years' enrollments are used to estimate statistically future years' enrollments. This procedure assumes that all student enrollments will be growing by the trend line in figure 4.3 (approximately thirty-eight students per year) and that any past or future differences from the trend line are relatively minor deviations from the prevailing long-term trend.

| Historical Enrollments | | Projected Enrollments | |
|---|---|---|---|
| Year | Students | Year | Students |
| 2012 | 13,142 | 2017 | 13,288 |
| 2013 | 13,029 | 2018 | 13,326 |
| 2014 | 13,195 | 2019 | 13,365 |
| 2015 | 13,309 | | |
| 2016 | 13,193 | | |

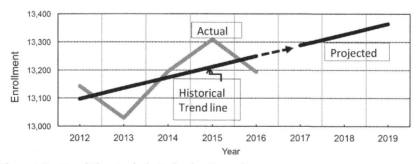

**Figure 4.3.  Trend Line Analysis Projection Example**

**Cohort Survival.** The most commonly used enrollment forecasting technique is cohort survival. This approach treats each grade level as a cohort, and the passage of students from one grade level to the next is followed through the school system from year to year. This is illustrated in figure 4.4 for a school district's elementary enrollments.

To follow the example, the initial cohort of 1,070 kindergarten students in 2011–2012 became the 1,065 first grade students in 2012–2013, and then were the 1,055 second grade students in 2013–2014, and so forth through their years in the district elementary program. The number of students

ELEMENTARY ENROLLMENTS

| Grade | 2011-12 | 2012-13 | 2013-14 | 2014-15 | 2015-16 | 2016-17 |
|-------|---------|---------|---------|---------|---------|---------|
| K | 1,070 | 1,091 | 1,027 | 1,005 | 1,018 | 993 |
| 1 | 1,006 | 1,065 | 1,088 | 976 | 986 | 1,038 |
| 2 | 963 | 995 | 1,055 | 1,037 | 954 | 974 |
| 3 | 997 | 955 | 993 | 1,029 | 1,084 | 969 |
| 4 | 978 | 980 | 953 | 949 | 1,063 | 1,073 |
| 5 | 992 | 949 | 988 | 939 | 982 | 1,073 |
| | | | | | | |
| K-5 | 6,006 | 6,035 | 6,104 | 5,935 | 6,087 | 6,120 |

SURVIVAL RATES

| Grade | 2011-12 | 2012-13 | 2013-14 | 2014-15 | 2015-16 | 2016-17 | 5 Year Average |
|-------|---------|---------|---------|---------|---------|---------|----------------|
| K | | | | | | | |
| 1 | | 0.995 | 0.997 | 0.950 | 0.981 | 1.020 | 0.989 |
| 2 | | 0.989 | 0.991 | 0.953 | 0.977 | 0.988 | 0.980 |
| 3 | | 0.992 | 0.998 | 0.975 | 1.045 | 1.016 | 1.005 |
| 4 | | 0.983 | 0.998 | 0.956 | 1.033 | 0.990 | 0.992 |
| 5 | | 0.970 | 1.008 | 0.985 | 1.035 | 1.009 | 1.002 |

ENROLLMENT PROJECTIONS

| Grade | Average Survival Ratio | Actual 2016-17 | Projected 2017-18 | Projected 2018-19 | Projected 2019-20 | Projected 3 Year Change |
|-------|------------------------|----------------|-------------------|-------------------|-------------------|-------------------------|
| K* | | 993 | 1,015 | 1,034 | 1,047 | 54 |
| 1 | 0.989 | 1,038 | 982 | 1,004 | 1,022 | (16) |
| 2 | 0.980 | 974 | 1,017 | 962 | 983 | 9 |
| 3 | 1.005 | 969 | 979 | 1,022 | 967 | (2) |
| 4 | 0.992 | 1,073 | 961 | 971 | 1,014 | (59) |
| 5 | 1.002 | 1,073 | 1,075 | 963 | 973 | (100) |
| | | | | | | |
| K-5 | | 6,120 | 6,029 | 5,955 | 6,006 | (114) |

\*   Kindergarten enrollments estimated independently from live birth data.

**Figure 4.4.   Cohort Survival Enrollment Projection Example**

enrolled in each grade level is shown for each of the past six years. Then a survival rate is calculated for each transition from one grade one year to the next grade next year. For example, the survival rate of kindergartners to first graders from 2011–2012 to 2012–2013 was 0.995 (1,065/1,070). Similar rates are calculated for each grade/year cell in the enrollment data matrix.

Using the various years' rates, we calculated an average for each grade-to-grade transition over the given time period. In the example, the five-year average survival rate for kindergarten to first grade was 0.989, which is the average of the individual survival rates of kindergarten to first grade from 2012–2013 to 2016–2017, which ranged from 0.950 to 1.020. Note that survival rates can be greater than one if the enrollments in a cohort grow from one year to the next.

This method does not trace individual children; it is only concerned with the aggregate numbers in each grade for each year. Not all of the children in the following grade were necessarily in the prior grade. Transfers into the next grade from outside the school system are common. When more students transfer into than leave the school system, the survival rate will be greater than 1.0. This was the case in several grades in the example. The average survival rates are then used to project future enrollments on a grade-by-grade basis. The actual enrollments in each grade in the final year of actual data are multiplied by their respective average survival rates and the results are the projected enrollments in each grade for the following year.

For example, the five-year average survival rate from kindergarten to first grade (0.989) is multiplied by the students in kindergarten in 2016–2017 (993) to obtain a projected enrollment of 982 in first grade for 2017–2018. For the next year, the five-year average survival rate for first grade to second grade (0.980) is multiplied by the number of projected students in first grade in 2017–2018 (982) to obtain a projected enrollment of 962 in second grade in 2018–2019.

One hole exists in the set of grade-level projections for the next year—the kindergarten. The projection for a given grade level is based on the students in the previous grade. The entry grade into the school—kindergarten in this example—has no prior grade or students from which to derive its projected enrollment. Therefore, it is necessary to estimate the enrollment in the entry grade separately. A similar statistical projection technique can be employed by calculating a series of survival ratios for the number of kindergarten students in a given year to the number of live births in the district's catchment area five years before.

The average of these ratios is then multiplied by the number of live births four years ago (five years prior to next year's kindergarten class) to obtain a projection of the number of kindergarten students for the upcoming year. This initial estimate can be adjusted from enrollment information from preschool programs in the district, estimates of the in- or out-migration of families, and data on new housing developments.

As with all extrapolation techniques, the cohort survival estimates become less secure the further out they are made. While the 2017–2018 projections in the example are based on the actual enrollments in the prior year, the projections in later years are based on projected rather than actual enrollments. Further, it assumes the conditions that prevailed in past years will continue into the future.

## RELIABILITY OF ENROLLMENT PROJECTIONS

The results from any enrollment projection methodology—the cohort survival method, trend line analysis, or others??—should not be automatically accepted as perfectly correct or accurate. As cautioned by a state department of education:

> Projection models of this nature are based on the concept that students progress routinely from one grade to another and that any internal policies and external factors that influenced grade progression in the past will continue to influence the progression of students from grade to grade in the future.[2]

Past conditions, such as annual survival rates, enrollment levels, or changes in enrollment levels, should be reviewed for deviations from the general grade level pattern. For example, in the cohort survival example, the third to fourth grade survival rate in 2015–2016 was 1.033, the only rate in that group greater than 1.0. In every other of past five years, there was a loss of students from third to fourth grade. An annual rate or enrollment level that seems out of line is not necessarily wrong, but it should be identified and possibly investigated to see if it was an aberrant condition or a normal difference.

Since the annual survival rate average is used as the multiplier in the projections, an abnormal year will distort the average rate and hence the projected enrollments. The same is true for enrollment levels in calculating the trend line equation.

A simple, but useful, data check is to observe *enrollment pattern trends*. A steadily increasing or decreasing rate of a grade level may indicate that past year's survival rate would be a more accurate indicator of next year's transition than the five-year average rate, which is based on historical information that may be different from expected future conditions. Where appropriate, the projection assumptions or results can be modified to reflect the expected future situation more accurately. This may be necessary when districts are

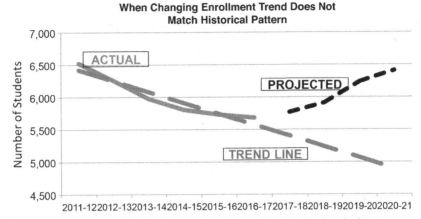

**Figure 4.5.  When Changing Enrollment Trend Does Not Match Historical Pattern**

facing significant changes, such as the end of a period of declining enrollments and the beginning of increasing enrollments.

Figure 4.5 illustrates what can happen if the past conditions do not continue
into the future projection period. In this case, the projection of continued
declines in enrollment would be incorrect if the reductions have come to an
end and are not recognized by the district. If enrollments do rise over the
next several years, program and budget plans based on past declining trends
would lead to shortages of teachers, classroom space, and insufficient revenue. This is not necessarily a hypothetical example as nationally the decline
in total secondary enrollments bottomed out in 1990 and began increasing in
the following year;[3] extrapolating from the preceding five years would have
indicated further declines and would have missed both the number of students
and the direction of change.

## Impact of Outdated Assumptions on Extrapolating Future Enrollments

Enrollment projections are less reliable for smaller populations. Changes in
residential conditions, demographic composition, and other characteristics
will have a larger impact on a smaller area. Relatively small changes in projection assumptions can have a much greater impact on projection results in
smaller school districts. With a smaller population and fewer schools than
larger districts, they have less ability to absorb inaccurate results in future
projection estimates. The potential for greater deviations can be even more
likely for individual neighborhoods and school attendance areas within a
school district.

More generally, underlying assumptions on which the projections are based should be examined for their continued reliability over the projection period. For example, the Great Recession yielded several emerging issues in school enrollment projections. With the loss of confidence in economic security, birth rates declined by as much as 30 percent in many communities from their highpoint in 2006 to 2008.

Neighborhood turnover stagnated as economic uncertainty kept some residents in their homes longer than planned and kept others from looking for new homes, despite record low mortgage rates. In some school systems the birth rates have rebounded, but generally not to the pre-recession levels. The long-term impact of lost confidence in the investment value of homeownership may also lead to different patterns of residential growth and neighborhood change.

Such longer-term changes in birth rates can have very significant changes on school district programs, budgets, and facilities. Figure 4.2 also illustrates the impact of an extended decrease in birth rates for a district. A 20 percent decrease in birth rates in a given year would in five years result in a corresponding drop in the number of students entering kindergarten. If the decline in birthrates continued, as this smaller number of students continued to enter into and progress through the school, the 20 percent drop in each grade would occur in each succeeding grade resulting in an overall decrease in the size of the school's enrollment.

The fewer students would require fewer teachers and other instructional personnel, not as many classrooms for instruction, lower levels of instructional supplies and equipment—and less state aid for any student-based subsidies. However, if the decline in birth rates proves to be a short-term phenomenon, then relatively minor adjustments could be made and the district would not overreact with long-term actions. Without monitoring birth rates in the district and schools' catchment areas, the district will be unprepared for its future and could make serious and costly mistakes regarding staffing levels and construction of new facilities.

Other economic or educational conditions can have substantial effects on school district enrollment, as well. As charter schools have become more widely available, more parents have been choosing to send their children to these new choices, which have reduced the number of students remaining in traditional public schools, and can have a significant financial impact on districts in some states. For example, in Pennsylvania, where school districts are required to pay the full cost of charter school tuition for their students (ranging from $10,000 per regular student to over $25,000 for special students), the total additional cost to districts statewide was $1.5 billion in 2015.[4]

Additionally, in some districts and states, some students who previously have been home-schooled have been added to the public school rolls, either in district classrooms or in charter schools; the transition changes the responsibility for supporting and providing instructional space for these new students from the parents to the school district. Ironically, another factor impacting the number of students in public schools is the affordability of private school tuitions. In good economic times more parents can choose to send their children to private schools, but in less prosperous times some parents may feel more inclined to use the public schools to avoid the tuition of private schooling.

## MANAGING CHANGING ENROLLMENTS

Adjusting to changing enrollments requires both annual and long-term planning. Fluctuations in enrollments from one school year to the next at a school or grade level can be significant. Annual review is required to adjust staffing levels for efficient and effective staff distribution among the district's schools. Planning of staffing levels in the spring and summer may not accurately predict the number of teachers needed in the fall due to last-minute enrollment changes and student movement within the district. While many school systems have some form of class size guidelines, it is difficult to adjust staffing levels downward due to contractual restrictions if projected enrollments do not materialize at the start of the school year.

On the other hand, it may be difficult to avoid adding staff if enrollments increase at a grade level or a program level, although some shifting of teaching assignments from one school to another may help alleviate the need for new staff. Demographic changes may also affect program enrollments in ELLs, special education populations, and other enrollments requiring specialized services. These services are often subject to class size and caseload regulations. Maintaining detailed records is necessary to provide data for program planning, implementation, and evaluation.

## ADVANCED TECHNOLOGICAL APPLICATIONS

New student information software systems allow for collection of many types of data for each student, as well as maintenance of historical information. Easy and timely access to these expanded data capabilities can be combined with a host of new technologies to provide more accurate and comprehensive enrollment analyses in a variety of areas. For example, school systems can maintain their own projections and update them regularly to incorporate the latest enrollment estimates throughout the budget process. Geographical information systems allow extensive capabilities to visualize enrollment data and correlate student data with demographic and economic information from other sources including the U.S. Census. Business intelligence software allows analysis of various large databases and visualization of that information in charts, graphs, and maps.

Student information systems can be expanded to include a variety of programmatic or personal data for individual students. For example, data fields in student records can be added for students enrolled in vocational education programs. This information would provide the data needed to project these enrollments in total numbers, by type of vocational program, and by school or other service location (e.g., separate career and technical education center) and develop the programs and plan the special resources needed for these populations.

Similar student data records could be established for special education by exceptionality, as well as for limited English-speaking proficiency, and other relevant student characteristics. With more detailed information maintained about each student, confidentiality of student records is paramount when using these data and is generally governed by the Family Educational Rights and Privacy Act (FERPA).[5]

Geographical information systems offer the potential to understand changing enrollment patterns and demographic changes. These systems allow visualization of any type of information included in student records through the use of geocodes identifying the latitude and longitude coordinates of each student's residency. School attendance area boundaries, U.S. Census boundaries, and school locations can also be shown on computer maps. The mapping capabilities allow visualization through color-coding of demographic factors by area boundaries. These systems can also show changes over time, such as the change in student population in a neighborhood.

The practical applications of geographic information on student enrollments are numerous. Enrollment change by neighborhood can be understood and displayed on maps. Demographic multipliers can be calculated for a specific neighborhood or region to determine the number of students received from various housing types in that school system. This can counteract the typical tendency to assume more students will result from a proposed residential development cause overbuilding of new school buildings. The grade level and educational program requirements of students can be mapped to allow programs to be assigned to school buildings that minimize travel time and cost.

Demographic and economic data from the U.S. Census can be correlated with student achievement data. Population projections performed by the U.S. Census can be compared with student enrollments by age cohorts, which can be shown by neighborhood. Mobility analysis can help understand the changes in enrollment within an attendance area. Census data can provide

**Figure 4.6. Gain/Loss in Population <5 Years Old**

information on students born but not in school yet to allow for time to plan the growth or declines in incoming students. As one example of the utility of these new tools, figure 4.6 compares the degree of gain or loss of preschool children in each of the census tracts in a school district and overlays the existing school locations.

The significant changes in preschool children in this example resulted from the impact of the Great Recession on birth rates and stagnant housing markets. This particular chart indicates that most of the existing schools are in areas with declining preschool students. This would provide important insight to the district about where near-future kindergarteners are coming from with implications of realigning attendance boundaries with the objective of balancing demographic factors among schools, bussing requirements, and the possible need for new schools in different locations that might replace some existing ones. Extensive enrollment and demographic data can be developed for use in grant applications and funding advocacy.

## CONCLUSION

Projecting future enrollments accurately is required for effective operations and financial management in school districts. While several different analytical techniques can be used for calculating the projections, the most common one is the *cohort survival method*. This approach determines the survival rate for each grade-to-grade/year-to-year progression of students through the school system and uses the average of these rates over several years to estimate future enrollments. Additional projections may be necessary to plan for separate subpopulations that have different educational programs and resource needs.

With all enrollment projection methods, it important to remember that the projections are based on the assumption that past conditions will remain in place for the future. Rather than taking enrollment projection results at face value, the basic underlying assumptions regarding historical enrollment trends, live birth rate trends, student demographic trends, housing develop-ments, economic activity in the community that could impact school enroll-ment, or changes in state and federal educational policies that could affect subgroup student populations and service requirements should be examined to insure that no significant changes are expected during the projected years.

Once the enrollment results have been satisfactorily established, they can be utilized by various administrators in the district to develop the detailed staffing, facilities, and other resource requirements along with the budget necessary to support the district's programs. Improvements in analytical software and database management coupled with utilization of geographical information systems provide better information each year for managing edu-cational programs. Analyzing more detailed student enrollment information gives administrators opportunities to plan more effectively for current opera-tions and to anticipate changes in staffing and facilities that may be necessary in the future.

## NOTES

1. For a discussion of enrollment projection techniques, see Crampton, Faith E., Craig Wood, R., & Thompson, David C. (2015). *Money and schools* (6th ed.). New York: Routledge, Ch. 5.

2. Pennsylvania Department of Education. *The enrollment projection model.* Available at http://www.education.pa.gov/Documents/Data%20and%20Statistics/Enrollment/Enrollment%20Projections/Enrollment%20Projections%20Model.pdf.

3. National Center for Educational Statistics, *Digest of educational statistics*, Table 203.10. Available at http://nces.ed.gov/programs/digest/current_tables.asp.

4. Pennsylvania Department of Education, *Tuition schedule 0304–1415.* Available at http://www.education.pa.gov/Teachers%20-%20Administrators/School%20Finances/Finances/AFR%20Data%20Summary/Pages/AFR-Data-Detailed-.aspx#.VZwC6mXD-Uk.

5. FERPA (20 U.S.C. § 1232g; 34 CFR Part 99) is a federal law that protects the privacy of student education records. Available at http://www2.ed.gov/policy/gen/guid/fpco/ferpa/index.html.

*Chapter 5*

# Personnel

## *Education Is a People Enterprise*

### Bruce S. Cooper and Stephen Coffin

## INTRODUCTION

Education finance is primarily about the varied costs of *personnel*: for example, people who teach, lead, and perform other tasks in and about the school and school system. As *About Education* explains:

> It truly does take an army to raise and educate a child. The most recognizable employees within a school district are the teachers. However, they represent only a portion of the personnel that works within the school. School personnel can be divided into three distinct categories including school leaders, faculty, and support staff. (p. 1)

Thus, school leaders need to understand the costs and pay levels for teachers (mainly), other administrators, and a range of support and maintenance staff in their schools. This chapter examines the costs, percentages, and skills necessary to manage, plan, and evaluate staff and their costs in schools.

### Understanding the Field of School Finances and Leadership

Let us start with a set of key definitions related to personnel and funding of staff and leaders in school systems. Here are some of the key definitions:

#### *Definitions*

A. "Certified school instructor" means a teacher or instructional support provider. These teachers and support staff are critical to the instruction and learning of the students.

B. "Certified school employee" or "certified school personnel" means a licensed school employee.

C. "Licensed school employee" means teachers, school administrators and instructional support providers.

D. "Instructional support provider" means a person who is employed to support the instructional program of a school district, including educational assistant, librarian, school counselor, social worker, school nurse, speech-language pathologist, psychologist, physical therapist, occupational therapist, recreational therapist, and interpreter for the deaf and diagnostician.

E. "Teacher" means a person who holds a level one, two or three-A license and whose primary duty is classroom instruction or the supervision, below the school principal level, of an instructional program.

F. "School employee" means licensed and non-licensed employees of the district.

G. "School Principal" means the chief instructional leader and administrative head of a public or private school.

H. "School Administrator" means a person licensed to administer in the district and includes school principal and central office administrators.

I. "Substitute Teacher" means a person who holds a state-issued certificate to substitute for a teacher in the classroom. According to an article in *EdNext*, teachers miss a small but regular number of days, about ten days, or 5 percent of the regular 180 days, requiring substitute teacher to be used. In particular,

> According to a 2009–2010 report from the U.S. Department of Education based on data from surveys of 57,000 schools, U.S. teachers take off an average of 9.4 days each or 5% of regular school days, during a typical 180-day school year, and substitute teachers are called to fill in for absent teachers. This means that the average public school student has substitute teachers for more than six months of his or her school career. In a new analysis, June Kronholz discusses recent research on teacher absences and the impact that the reliance on substitutes has on school budgets and student learning. (Kronholz, 2013, p. 3)

"Discharge" means the act of severing the employment relationship with a certified school employee prior to the expiration of the current employment contract.

K. "Terminate" means, in the case of a certified school employee, the act of not reemploying an employee for the ensuring school year and, in the case of a non-certified school employee, the act of severing the employment relationship with the employee.

As William J. Fowler (2017) explains,

Most educators readily acknowledge that schools districts in different geo-graphic locations encounter *different costs* in acquiring and retaining similarly qualified [and high quality] teachers. Teacher salaries reflect not only the cost-of-living in a geographic labor market, but also a school district's preference for teachers who are better education or more experienced. (2017, p. 2)

And here is a summary of the cost and effects of substitute teachers:

- Duke researchers Charles Clotfelter, Helen Ladd, and Jacob Vigdor found that being taught by a substitute for ten days per year has a larger effect on a child's math scores than if the child changed schools, and about half the size of the difference between students from well-to-do and poor families.
- Columbia University researchers Mariesa Herrmann and Jonah Rockoff (2011) concluded that the effect of learning to use a substitute for even a day is greater than the effect of replacing an average teacher with a terrible one—that is, a teacher in the 10th percentile for math instruction and the 20th percentile in English instruction.

These and other recent studies find that:

- Teachers in bigger schools were absent more often than those in smaller schools.
- Teachers in low-income schools were absent more often than those serving higher-income families.
- Elementary school teachers took off more time than did those in high schools.
- Tenured teachers took off 3.7 more days than did those without tenure.
- Female teachers under age thirty-five averaged 3.2 more absences than did men.
- Teachers who had a master's degree or graduated from a competitive col-lege took less leave then those who did not.
- Teachers in traditional districts take off more time than those in charters. About 37 percent of teachers are absent more than ten days at district ele-mentary and middle schools compared to 22 percent at charters.

Many school systems are plagued with dysfunctional human resources management systems. To understand how this dysfunction impacts the quality of education and school finance, we must understand the impact on schools, students, teachers, and administrators. Examples of the dysfunction include:

- Pay checks arrive late;
- Pay checks contain wrong amounts;

- People who are not on payroll getting paid;
- Performance evaluations may not reflect true performance;
- Poor or inaccurate or inadequate recordkeeping.

Subsequently, we must ask "How do these problems impact":

- Recruitment?
- Hiring?
- Development?
- Compensation especially in terms of "Pay for Performance?"
- Retaining Talent?

Finally, we must find possible solutions.

Possible solutions include the following: First, cast a wide net and do not allow top talent to get away. We can seek talent from these major sources:

- National organizations with reputation for recruiting and training top talent educators and administrators such as:
- New Teacher Project
- Teach for America
- New School Leaders for New Schools
- Broad Foundation Urban School Leaders Program
- Academy for Urban School Leadership and
- Peace Corps
- Universities that educate and train top teachers, principals, and administrators such as:

  - Montclair State University
  - Columbia University
  - Syracuse University
  - CUNY—City University of New York provides tuition reimbursement for teachers who become certified in math and science.

The second possible solution is having the Human Resources Department use online services to become a true "Customer-Service Center." Use online systems to automate the application and selection process. Link these processes to payroll systems to save time, money, and improve customer service to help to retain, attract, and hire talent.

The third possible solution is to focus on rigorous training and retention because nationwide about 30 percent of new teachers leave the profession within the first five years. We can address this problem by providing sound mentoring especially for new hires. We must link benchmarks to state teaching standards.

The fourth possible solution is that we must maintain sound leadership, especially at the top. We must maintain sustainable and continuous district leadership. Schools must hire and retain top superintendent and business administrators. Moreover, district leaders must forge and maintain strong links to the local community and government.

The fifth possible solution is that schools must get unions and district leadership to work together and achieve long-term collaboration. Some of the ways to accomplish this collaboration is to work together to lobby state and federal governments to fully fund all mandates.

## CONCLUSION

If a district wants to attract, hire, develop, and retain the best talent possible, then the Human Resources Department must be state of the art. The Human Resources Departments must use up-to-date technology because hiring the top talent in the twenty-first century requires the use of twenty-first-century technology and tools. Schools might consider teacher performance pay that is in practice or under discussion in many states. However, the most common approach is test-based pay for performance.

We must examine the underlying assumptions such as somehow teachers will try harder if they are motivated by the chance to earn additional money. But this assumes teachers are not trying hard now! It also assumes that teachers somehow know what to do but simply are not or will not perform at a higher level without the prospect of more money.

However, this assumes that teachers are motivated more by money than meeting their students' educational needs. This begs the following questions: (1) How do we define performance pay? (2) How do we know that students actually are learning more simply by scoring higher or well on state-wide tests? (3) What other criteria can be used beside money to incentivize teachers and teaching? A pay for performance compensation system requires definition before it is implemented. Schools must understand what students and teachers think about this.

Hence, a district must determine what it seeks to accomplish with performance pay system and how all affected employees will contribute to and meet the goals. Most importantly, if performance pay is based on student performance then student performance must also be defined. Measures of student performance must be developed which answer these questions:

- Do scores on standardized tests indicate any of the student's skill level, knowledge, or ability to succeed in life and contribute to society?

- If these points are true, then how do we create students who are:

  - life-long learners,
  - have the skills to succeed in life,
  - are critical thinkers,
  - have "twenty-first-century" skills,
  - are problem solvers, and
  - who reach their full potential.

Then students can pursue different paths in life based on their individual interests and abilities.

## Going Forward: The Necessity of Keeping Good Leaders

Besides the quality and value to schools of good teachers, we should also be aware of the need for good leaders to remain in their jobs within their schools, and the costs of replacing a school principal, the key leader at the building level (see ASCD *SmartBrief* October 31, 2014). A study found that leader-turnover was a critical problem in schools: "Some of those principals left on their own. Some were removed. According to a new report from the nonprofit School Leaders Network, half of new principals quit in their third year on the job."

And as one teacher reported, "Heather Wolpert-Gawron has been teaching for eleven years at Jefferson Middle School in San Gabriel, Calif. During that time, she says, the school has had about ten principals. The group, which provides training and support to principals, says the job has become too complex and isolating. Principals put in long hours overseeing teachers, meeting with parents and implementing one reform after another."

## REFERENCES

Analysis/Methodology Report (October 1995). *Public school teacher cost differences across the United States*. Washington, DC: About Education, 2017.

Chambers, J., Jr., & Fowler, W. J. (2017). *A comprehensive breakdown of the roles of school personnel*. Washington, DC: American Institutes for Research, National Center for Education Statistics.

Herrmann, M. A., & Rockoff, J. E. (2011). Worker absence and productivity: Evidence from teaching. *Journal of Labor Economics*, *122* (561), pp. 49–82.

Kronholz, J. (02/06/2013). "Substitute Teachers Are a Large Presence in American Schools." *Education Next*.

Scott, A. (2014). *The high cost of principal turnover. Smart-briefs* (pp. 34–38). Washington, DC: ASCD.

*Chapter 6*

# Special Education

## *Special Needs Budgeting*

### Stephen Coffin and Bruce S. Cooper

IDEA (i.e., Individuals with Disabilities in Education Act) is the chief legislative and mandated program and service driver for special education. However, IDEA has been underfunded since its inception in 1975. Although President Obama promised full funding of IDEA, he did not seek or get full funding. The president's FY2017 budget funds IDEA at FY2016 levels of only 16 percent of the full cost of all IDEA special education-mandated programs and services.

Underfunding IDEA at only 16 percent is less than half of the federal government's original 40 percent limit on funding students with educational and physiological disabilities. Moreover, the federal government promised to pay only 40 percent of the national average per special education pupil expenditure penalizing districts with higher-than-average per-pupil special education expenditures. The highest funding level provided by the federal government for IDEA's mandated programs and services was 18 percent in 2005. This means that President Obama's proposed funding level for FY2017 is below that of more than a decade ago under President Bush.

National funding IDEA at only 16 percent means 84 percent must be paid for by local and state public school districts nationwide because IDEA's programs and services are mandated. Mandated programs and services require any funding deficit to be funded by public school districts. Therefore, underfunding IDEA requires districts to make up for the funding shortfall by cutting nonmandate-protected programs and services. Underfunding IDEA is one of the most powerful drivers of public school district budget cuts nationwide. Moreover, the chronic underfunding of IDEA and the budget cuts it fosters often pit regular and special education parents, students, and teachers against one another in a battle for scarce financial, material, and human educational resources.

—**Key Question:** *Why should not the federal government be required to pay 100 percent of its special education policy mandates?*

**Answer:** Special education expenses are one of the fastest growing financial challenges confronting school districts nationwide—and particularly in New Jersey. School districts throughout New Jersey pay not only all of the general expense for their special education students but also the majority of the "excess cost" of special education. "Excess cost" is defined as the per-pupil cost of special education that exceeds the regular student cost. Declining state and federal aid not only has increased the proportion of property taxes used to fund schools but also has heightened the pressure to find necessary resources perhaps by reducing programs and services for regular education students in order to fund mandate-protected programs and services such as special education.

Special education costs are driven primarily by expensive out-of-district placements; by mandated preschool programs, including intensive services for autistic students; by lower special education student-to-staff ratios; and by parents suing school districts to obtain private school placements for their children. The legal fees for such law suits account for another escalating expense for schools. In addition, if a school district loses in a New Jersey administrative court, the district not only has to pay the judgment costs but also has to pay all of the plaintiff's legal costs regardless of the length of the trial. It seems as if holding New Jersey school districts harmless from such law suits would be another way to enable school districts to allocate more of their scarce resources to instruction.

Many districts find that out-of-district placements can consume as much as 50 percent of the special education budget. The students placed in out-of-district schools tend to be the most expensive because they are usually the children most in need of special educational programs and services. Depending on the student's disability, the annual cost of sending a student to an out-of-district private school can range from roughly $60,000 to over $250,000—especially for the most educationally and physically challenged students.

The federal government forces its traditional public schools to pay for an ever-increasing proportion of special education costs by underfunding IDEA mandates. IDEA's underfunding forces districts to increase local property taxes and identify funds to offset the shortfall through means that adversely impact the regular education budget. Underfunded IDEA mandates can result in much larger class sizes as school districts are forced to consider reducing regular education teachers and aides. Larger class sizes often lead to lower test scores, which make it more difficult for students, schools, and districts to achieve academic progress.

And each new administration may have a different view of the federal role: President Trump is a good current example, as one source reports:

That blueprint includes reducing so-called formula funding in education by 10 percent, or $2.3 billion, for federal programs like Title I whose aid is allotted mainly according to fixed formulas; cutting competitive and project grant funding under the Every Student Succeeds Act by $1.8 billion; and phasing out Head Start by cutting 10 percent from the program each year, or $935 million in the first year. (Head Start, which serves preschoolers from poor families, is overseen by the Department of Health and Human Services, not the Education Department.)

In the current year's budget, Title I for disadvantaged students is the largest single piece of federal K-12 spending, at $14.9 billion, followed by Individuals with Disabilities Education

Act state grants, at $11.9 billion. (Ujifusa, February 7, 2017, p. 3)

Although the Heritage budget calls for a 10 percent cut to formula-funded educational programs, the director of the think tank's Center for Education Policy, Lindsey Burke, said it wants to look at allocating IDEA money differently but is not calling for cuts in that aid at this time.

Unless public school districts nationwide not only wish to avoid IDEA-driven continued budget cuts to offset IDEA's underfunding and a downward spiral in the quality of education stemming from IDEA's underfunding but also wish for higher property taxes, then the districts nationwide should ban together and demand that the federal government fund IDEA 100 percent, and therefore, pay for all of the costs of IDEA's mandated programs and services. Moreover, fully funding IDEA would prevent the budget cuts it currently fosters. Stopping IDEA-driven budget cuts would end the conflict among regular and special education parents, students, and teachers over scarce financial, material, and human educational resources and put the focus on working together to provide a quality education for all.

IDEA reauthorization is seven years past due. Even with the 84 percent underfunding of IDEA, the federal government's Special Educational program mandates that local education agencies (LEAs), local school districts, fund the unfunded portion or 84 percent. Many scholars, particularly Dr. Bruce Baker (2011), have found that the federal under-funding of IDEA drives budget gaps and causes other non-mandate- protected programs and services to be cut, especially in large urban districts.!

Let us focus our Special Ed in this chapter on IDEA, and how its 84 percent under-funding drives other budgetary shortfalls in districts! IDEA needs *reauthorization* and *full funding*; both will help districts avoid severe budget cuts and staff reductions!

# REFERENCES

Baker, B. D. (February 4, 2011). *Where's the pork? Mitigating the damage of state aid cuts* [Web log post]. Available at http://www.schoolfinance101.wordpress.com.

Ujifusa, A. (February 7, 2017). "Big Stakes for K-12 as Federal Budget Process Gears Up," *Education Week*, pp. 1–3.

*Chapter 7*

# State Education Aid

## *How to Budget and Manage State Aid*

### Stephen Coffin and Bruce S. Cooper

### INTRODUCTION

Because education is primarily a state responsibility—according to the U.S. Constitution and the fifty states' constitutions—the nation has fifty different educational systems. Laws, curricula, standards, school organization, and testing are in part set by the state legislatures, governors, courts, and state education agencies—and carried out in the nation's approximately 14,000 local school systems. As the U.S. Census reported in 2012,

> School districts are public school systems that provide regular, special, and/or vocational education services for children in pre-kindergarten through 12th grade. Public school systems in the United States are locally administrated, and their geographic structure varies by state and region. Most districts in the Mid-Atlantic and New England states follow county, township, or city boundaries, while districts in the Midwest and Western states are generally independent of municipal boundaries and frequently intersect statistical areas like Census tracts and block groups. The U.S. has more than 14,000 public school districts and spends more than $500 billion on public elementary and secondary education each year (combined spending of federal, state, and local governments).

While the states are all under the U.S. Constitution—for example, national laws and regulations, and receive 11 percent from federal funding—the structure and operation of schools have mostly been left to the states, which now pay the *second-largest percentage of total education funding—with local and federal funding coming in most cases at a lower percentage and level.* Each state must "raise the money" through taxation, and then divvy it up among the local school districts (except Hawaii which is a one statewide district), and set goals, performance levels, testing, and outcomes.

Thus, states are quite different, in some ways, concerning how they raise and use funds for K-12 education. This chapter examines various attempts to equalize school funding across and within the fifty states and the District of Columbia. Two states are perhaps the most different. For example, Hawaii has local district funding at a high level with $5.9 billion state spending and $3.8 billion local, while Hawaii has no direct local funding or governance of schools at all, with one state school system, one school board, and school superintendent (statewide), and thus one education budget in Honolulu for the whole state.

Hawaii has little local funding (only $3.0 billion raised locally); no local elections; and no local school boards or superintendents of schools, with the state contributing $11 billion toward schools. Odd, because Hawaii is also the most physically and geographically divided state in the United States, with four different islands, separated by the Pacific Ocean. As the Roth reports in Hawaii:

> The *Hawaii State Department of Education* is the only statewide public educa-
> tion system in the United States. The school district can be thought of as analo-
> gous to the school districts of other cities and communities in the United States,
> but in some manners can also be thought of as analogous to the state education
> agencies of other states. As the official state education agency, the Hawaii State
> Department of Education oversees all 283 public schools and charter schools
> and over 13,000 teachers in the State of Hawaii. (Roth, September 3, 2015,
> pp. 1–8)

To understand the differences among the fifty states in the governance and funding of schools, we raise these issues and questions: "To do this, we first classify governance relative to three main components:

—The degree to which decision-making authority lies at the state versus the local level.
—The degree is decision-making authority distributed among many institu-
tions versus consolidated in a few" (Zeehandelaar et al., 2015, p. 3).
—The degree to which the public can participate in the policy-making process.

We score states on each component, then combine them into eight "gover-
nance types" named for the characteristics they have in common with some of history's most famous political leaders and theorists.

So while all states are bound by federal laws, policies, and programs, each state sets its own organizational, financial models, levels and types of taxation, and, thus, has different amounts, rankings, and per-pupil levels of resources. Table 7.1 shows the fifty states in terms of per-pupil spending, based on financial income and number of students.

**Table 7.1. Spending by Fifty States on Education (in Trillions of Dollars in 2015)**

| State ▼ | State Revenue ($) | Local Revenue ($) |
| --- | --- | --- |
| Alabama | 21.0 | 15.0 |
| Alaska | 6.9 | 2.7 |
| Arizona | 24.8 | 20.5 |
| Arkansas | 15.7 | 3.9 |
| California | 262.7 | 184.2 |
| Colorado | 24.7 | 22.4 |
| Connecticut | 28.3 | 14.4 |
| Delaware | 7.7 | 2.1 |
| District of Columbia | −0.2 | 10.0 |
| Florida | 74.4 | 67.6 |
| Georgia | 37.4 | 29.2 |
| Hawaii | 11.0 | 3.0 |
| Idaho | 7.1 | 3.3 |
| Illinois | 64.5 | 46.2 |
| Indiana | 26.2 | 16.6 |
| Iowa | 15.9 | 10.6 |
| Kansas | 13.7 | 9.5 |
| Kentucky | 20.0 | 9.7 |
| Louisiana | 21.0 | 29.0 |
| Maine | 6.4 | 2.6 |
| Maryland | 32.0 | 21.7 |
| Massachusetts | 41.8 | −2.6 |
| Michigan | 49.4 | 25.4 |
| Minnesota | 40.1 | 20.1 |
| Mississippi | 13.2 | 8.4 |
| Missouri | 23.4 | 18.6 |
| Montana | 5.9 | 2.4 |
| Nebraska | 7.9 | 11.0 |
| Nevada | 12.2 | 8.1 |
| New Hampshire | 5.9 | 3.8 |
| New Jersey | 50.1 | 36.9 |
| New Mexico | 11.2 | 3.9 |
| New York | 137.3 | 124.7 |
| North Carolina | 45.7 | 32.6 |
| North Dakota | 9.4 | 2.3 |
| Ohio | 58.4 | 34.9 |
| Oklahoma | 18.0 | 10.0 |
| Oregon | 22.9 | 12.7 |
| Pennsylvania | 62.4 | 37.3 |
| Rhode Island | 6.1 | 4.0 |
| South Carolina | 20.3 | 13.9 |
| South Dakota | 3.3 | 2.5 |
| Tennessee | 22.8 | 24.8 |
| Texas | 109.5 | 93.8 |

*(Continued)*

**Table 7.1.    (Continued)**

| State ▼ | State Revenue ($) | Local Revenue ($) |
|---|---|---|
| **All States Combined** | *1,648.3* | *1,159.7* |
| Utah | *12.6* | *8.1* |
| Vermont | *4.9* | *1.2* |
| Virginia | *37.8* | *25.5* |
| Washington | *37.4* | *27.8* |
| West Virginia | *9.6* | *3.5* |
| Wisconsin | *30.6* | *18.7* |
| *Wyoming* | *4.6* | *3.4* |
| **All States Combined, 2015** | *$1,648.3 billion* | *$1,159.7 billion* |
| **TOTAL: STATE AND LOCAL: $ 2.8 TRILLION.** | | |

## Funding

As we saw in the previous chapter, approximately 44 percent of a school district's revenue comes from local funds, primarily from property taxes. States are a major source of revenue for schools, contributing the overall level of school resources. States have the authority to levy a variety of taxes in the form of personal and corporate income taxes, general sales taxes, motor fuel taxes, utility taxes, and alcohol and tobacco taxes, to name the major ones. In most cases, this tax money is placed in a general revenue fund to be distributed to a multitude of competing governmental bodies, including public schools.

How much revenue public schools receive from the state depends on the state. Some states have constitutionally mandated amounts that go to public education. For example, a state constitution may mandate that 25 percent of the state's general revenue must be allocated to education. According to the NCES report in the school year 2010–2011, in twenty states, at least half of education revenues came from state governments, a rather significant amount. Nationally, schools received an average of 44 percent in the school year 2010–2011 from state sources, a decrease from the 50 percent in the school year 2000–2001.

Thus, we are truly the United States of America in educational provision, with each state being its own educational system and funding. When comparing state revenues for education with local revenues (see table 7.1), we see the degree to which most school systems depend on state aid, in addition to the local spending levels. Overall, in 2015, the United States spent $1,648.3 billion from state sources, total, and $1.159.7 billion from local sources (mostly from local property taxes). Total at the state and local levels of spending on public education, K-12, was $2.8 trillion in the United States in 2015.

Only three states—Tennessee, Louisiana, and Nebraska—are different, as their spending percentage and level are higher locally than at the state level; or perhaps the statement should be: local spending in these three states in 2015 was and is higher than the state contributions.

As Kenyon explained:

Property taxation and school funding are closely linked in the United States, with nearly half of all property tax revenue used for public elementary and secondary education. There is an active policy debate across the country regarding the degree to which public schools should be funded with property tax dollars. Some policy makers and analysts call for reduced reliance on property tax revenue and increased reliance on state funding; others claim that the property tax is a critical ingredient in effective local government. School funding is no less controversial, and nearly every state has dealt with school funding litigation and court mandates at least once over the last several decades. (Kenyon, 2007, p. 1)

The major plans for distributing state revenue include some type of foundation formula, guaranteed tax base, equalizing formula, or combination thereof. Since no two state plans for distributing revenue are the same, it is not feasible to discuss all the plans. Plus, with the current trend of litigation regarding adequate and equitable funding, plans are often subject to change.

## Federal Sources

Meanwhile, the U.S. (federal) spending on K-12 education has stayed fairly stable over the past fifty or so years, as shown in figure 7.1.

In this chapter we will examine the concept of distributing money based on adequacy and equity. Many plans incorporate local wealth factors and some form of student attendance, whether it is average daily attendance or average daily membership. School leaders understand that students' daily attendance is important for the student educationally. Understanding how the state aid distribution formula works can help shape policies that encourage school attendance, thereby increasing funding to the school.

In summary, states are less able to support local K-12 education since the recession, as this report explains:

At least thirty states are providing less funding per student for the 2014–2015 school year than they did before the recession hit. Fourteen of these states have cut per-student funding by more than 10 percent. (These figures, like all the comparisons in this chapter, are in inflation-adjusted dollars and focus on the primary form of state aid to local schools.)

Most states are providing more funding per student in the new school year than they did a year ago, but funding has generally not increased enough to make up for cuts in past years. For example, Alabama is increasing school

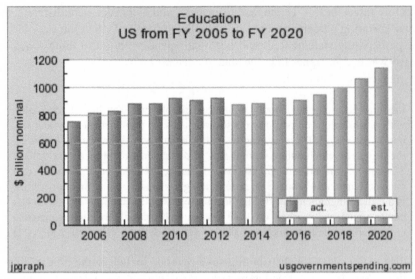

**Figure 7.1.   US School Spending, 2005 to 2020, Estimated**

funding by $16 per pupil this year. But that is far less than is needed to offset the state's $1,144 per-pupil cut over the previous six years (Leachman and Mai, 2014, pp. 1–2).

### State's Role in Education

The United States has fifty states and fifty different education systems, as each state established its own education system. And, education is fundamentally a state responsibility and matter, which means the schools of the United States are very different from each other under federal laws and court cases. For example, the state determines the governance systems for itself. And the differences are extreme and interesting.

For example, Hawaii has only one "school district"—and thus one statewide school board and superintendent. This is unusual, given that Hawaii is the physically most broken-up state, with five islands separated by the Pacific Ocean. Figure 7.2 below shows the state differences in school district funding (Leachman and Mai, 2014).

At the other extreme New Hampshire which had $8.4 billion spent in 2014 at the *local level*, and only $4.8 billion at the *state level*, with many local school districts among the lowest state taxes and state control of education in the country. Thus, the local boards and superintends have the most authority, and the state "leaves it to the districts" to set and pay for their own programs. The remaining forty-eight states have different blends of local and state control, with overall the state having the final authority on most issues. And each state has its own balance.

Overall, then, we see the fifty states contributing $1.65 trillion in total to K-12 education, with the local district levels at $1.26 billion, overall in 2014. The United States thus spends about $2.9 trillion on education, not counting the federal dollars.

## Federal Spending on Education

The federal government provided only $140 billion to education, and even that small amount is tough to analyze because of the distance from Washington to state capitals to local districts, to local schools. As explained, we're talking about 2014 spending.

> Calculating that figure is challenging. Federal programs administered by the U.S. Department of Education appear in two separate parts of the federal budget, and other agencies administer large programs as well. Furthermore, measuring spending on the federal student loan program is not straightforward, and the government provides significant subsidies for higher education in the form of tax benefits.

Therefore, the $141 billion figure includes the annual appropriation for the U.S. Department of Education, spending for the U.S. Department of Education not subject to annual appropriations (i.e. mandatory spending), school meal programs administered by the U.S. Department of Agriculture, the Head Start program in the Departments of Health and Human Services, the forgone revenue and spending on education tax benefits for individuals, and military and veterans education benefits.

The federal government spent a total of $3.5 trillion in FY2013. That means the approximate $141 billion in education spending accounts for approximately 4 percent of the entire federal budget (Leachman and Mai, 2014, pp. 1–2).

## Level of Funding

In 2011, Governor Jerry Brown of California advocated a shift in his state's governance system for education:

> Governor Jerry Brown's January 2011 budget proposal suggests shifting responsibility and funding for many state programs from the state to the local level. Under this "realignment" of government authority, local governments—usually counties—would be given responsibility for providing the services in realigned programs, and the state would provide local governments with a

source of funding for the new responsibilities. In addition, local governments would be granted the authority to reshape realigned programs to better accommodate local conditions and priorities. (Weston, 2011, p. 1)

Thus, the U.S. Department of Education (2013) states that the U.S. Constitution leaves the responsibility for public K-12 education primarily with the states, as explained:

The responsibility for K-12 education rests with the states under the U.S. Constitution. There is also a compelling national interest in the quality of the nation's public schools. Therefore, the federal government, through the legislative process, provides assistance to the states and schools in an effort to supplement, not supplant, and state support. The primary source of federal K-12 support began in 1965 with the enactment of the Elementary and Secondary Education Act (ESEA).

As Augenblick, Myers, and Anderson (2014) explain and compare "equity," "equitability," and "equality":

As we define "equity" in school funding, we must also consider the companion term, "equality." Both terms have a place in our discussion, we should understand that funding can be equal, but no "equitable," since the second term means "fair." And funding all schools and students the same may not be "fair" since some students deserve and need more funding. Ensuring equity and equality or adequacy of education funding is two of the most complex problems facing state legislatures. Not only are the concepts of equity and adequacy difficult to measure and to implement, but every state must meet the needs of a large number of school districts, which usually vary considerably in their student characteristics and needs (such as student need for compensatory or special education), costs of doing business (for example, teacher salary schedules and benefits or building and land acquisition costs), ability and willingness to raise local tax revenues, and local preferences for educational services (such as vocational training requiring expensive specialized equipment or advanced placement college-preparatory courses). (pp. 6–8)

Starting with the *Serrano v. Priest* (1971) case in California, high poverty districts have sued for greater state aid and greater equity. The California Supreme Court ruled that (Brimley, Verstegen, and Garfield, 2012):

California's method of funding public education, because of district-to-district disparities, "fails to meet the requirements of the equal protection clause of the Fourteenth Amendment of the United States Constitution and the California Constitution." . . . "[As] a direct result of the financing scheme they are required to pay a higher tax rate than [taxpayers] in many other school districts in order to obtain for their children the same or lesser educational opportunities afforded children in those other districts."

That is, an actual controversy has arisen and now exists between the parties as to the validity and constitutionality of the financing scheme under the Fourteenth Amendment of the U.S. Constitution and under the California Constitution.

As Brimley, Verstegen, and Garfield (2012) explain, the California Supreme Court found that "the school finance system with its uneven tax burden and disparate spending patterns were unconstitutional" (p. 177). Thus, the case and following pressures reduced local (unequal) school funding from two-thirds to one-quarter, thus forcing the state to contribute more and a higher percentage to education in California.

In summary, the differences between "property rich" and "property poor" districts were quite large in 1971—the year of *Serrano* decision in California— with rich districts such as Beverly Hills having $50,885 per student valuation; the basis of taxing, and poor districts such as Baldwin Park with only $3,706 per student, on which taxation could be made (a rich-to-poor ratio of 14 to 1). Thus, even though residents and businesses in poor districts like Baldwin Park paid higher tax levels, they were unable to raise sufficient funds without state aid. So, even with poor district residents and business paying higher taxes on their property, the district obtained less funding, given the lower value of taxable businesses and homes (see Brimley, Verstegen, and Garfield, 2012, p. 215).

Most recently, equity groups representing the 600 Texas school districts in 2011 brought a suit against the state for greater equity among districts:

The case, *Texas Taxpayer & Student Fairness Coalition* (TTSFC) v. *State*, was filed by more than 600 Texas school districts in 2011 in response to a $5.4 billion cut in K-12 education funding by the state government. The plaintiff school districts in TTSFC educate 75 percent of the state's five million public school students. The school districts were represented by the Equity Center, the Mexican American Legal Defense and Educational Fund (MALDEF), and others.

The ruling provides a remedy to what has become a troubling pattern of denying adequate funding to low-income and minority students in states across the country. It comes on the heels of similar school funding cases in Kansas (*Gannon v. the State of Kansas*) and Washington (*McCleary v. State of Washington*) and pending cases in New York, Connecticut, and Colorado. The *Texas Taxpayer & Student Fairness Coalition* ruling is especially significant because 10 percent of all public school students in the nation are enrolled in Texas schools.

Thus, each school leader—state by state, district by district, and school by school—should know the local and state funding levels, equity, and ways to secure the most local, state, and federal funding. State funding is important, yet variable; thus leaders, particularly principals, should keep tabs on the level of school funding, district by district, and understand the levels from the federal, state, and local levels.

## Recommendations

This chapter has outlined and discussed the key roles of the state governments in funding local schools. As such, we have five recommendations for building leaders concerning this funding source:

1. **Know and keep abreast of state programs and policies that will affect funding levels and programs in each school.** We have shown the critical role and importance of states in supporting education. Thus, school administrators should keep in touch with their local state representatives and agencies, to be informed about state aid, whether it is basic funding or special funding for students with learning and personal problems. Local elected representatives are usually open to inquiries and requests from school leaders in their communities and districts.
2. **Be responsive.** But these leaders and agencies can only respond if they are informed and lobbied by educators in schools they serve. Monthly meetings with these politicians and bureaucrats make sense: build a relationship and be supportive but be also demanding, based on the needs of schools and local kids. If they do not know, they will be unlikely to act in the best interest of their schools, leaders, teachers, and students.
3. **Keep in touch with state representatives—those locally elected leaders, who can explain how new laws can benefit our schools.** Work with colleagues to show interest and solidarity around key issues. If a state aid package comes up for consideration, which local leaders like, band together and show shared force and influence, which leads to their next recommendation:
4. **Let each school administrator association and union know what the school's needs are and work to influence these groups to develop influence with state governors, legislatures, and education officials.** Principals have their own associations and unions, sometimes affiliated with the American Federation of School Administrators—and with the AFL-CIO; try to pull these large and more powerful groups into the fray: to lobby for, get, and use additional resources from the state.

Cowen and Strunk (2014) state that unions in education can matter in setting state policies, as follows:

> Focusing on unions' role in shaping education policy, we argue that collective bargaining and political organizing comprise the two central but distinct forms

of influence at the district, state and national levels of decision-making. We note recent changes in state policy directly and indirectly affecting unions and union priorities. We argue that these changes may result in a variety of different conditions under which unions operate, and suggest that this variation represents fertile ground for new empirical analyses of union influence. Such work may in turn require a reconsideration of the extent of, and limitations to union power in altered educational landscapes. (p. 21)

5. **Keep a close eye on the state courts, as they often handle school finance issues and cases, to avoid—where possible—making things worse, and to understand the changing legal environment of schools and education affecting one's district and school.** Finally, we realize that the local and state judicial systems play major roles play in shaping education policies. The major cases include the *Brown* decision (1954) that helped to desegregate U.S. public schools, most intensively in the South and urban school districts across the country and the *Serrano* decision in California that started the movement to fund schools and students more equally and equitably.

Then, too, as we have discussed, state courts have often ruled in favor of greater school financial equality, by forcing the states to step in to fund high-need lower-property wealth schools. Each school administrator should keep up with funding, per pupil, compared to other schools in other districts. More equity (fairness) often means more funding for schools, in lower-income communities. As Bruce D. Baker (2014) explained, based on the national Equity and Excellence Commission, "For Each and Every Child":

Accordingly, this commission believes the time has come for bold action by the states—and the federal government—*to redesign and reform the funding of our nation's public schools*. The deep inequities in school funding documented by another federal commission more than 40 years ago . . . remain entrenched across our nation's states and school districts at a time when more than 40 percent of all American public school children are enrolled in districts of concentrated student poverty. (U.S. Department of Education, 2013, p. 25)

## REFERENCES

Augenblick, J. G., Myers, J. L., & Andersen, A. B. (1997). Equity and adequacy in school funding: The future of school funding. *Financing schools*, 7(3), pp. 1–16.

Baker, B. D. (2014). *America's most financially disadvantaged school districts and how they got that way: How state and local governance causes school funding disparities*. Washington, DC: Center for American Progress.

Cowen, J., & Strunk, K. O. (2014). *How do teachers' unions influence education policy? What we know and what we need to learn*. Lansing, MI: Michigan State University Graduate School of Education.

Kenyon, D. A. (December 2007). *The property tax-school funding dilemma (policy focus report)*. Phoenix, AZ: Lincoln Institute of Land Policy.

Leachman, M., & Mai, C. (May 20, 2014). *Most states funding schools less than before the recession*. Center on Budget and Policy Priorities.

Roth, R. W. (2015). *Public education in Hawai'i: Past, present & future*. Honolulu, HA: Governor Office.

U.S. Bureau of the Census. (2013). *Public school system finance*. Washington, DC: American FactFinder.

U.S. Department of Education. (June 2008). *About education: 10 facts about K-12 funding*. Washington, DC: U.S. Department of Education.

U.S. Department of Education. (2013). *For each and every child—A strategy for education equity and excellence*. Washington, DC: U.S. Department of Education.

Weston, M. (2011). *Rethinking the state-local relationship: K—12 education*. Sacramento, CA: Public Policy of California.

Zeehandelaar, D., Griffith, D. et al. with David Griffith, David, Smith, Joanna, Thier, Michael, Anderson, Ross, Pitts, Christine, & Gasparian, Hovanes. (August 2015). *Schools of thought: A taxonomy of American education governance*. Washington, DC: Heartland Institute.

*Chapter 8*

# Budgeting and Managing Federal Aid for Schools

## Stephen Coffin and Bruce S. Cooper

The federal government's role in, and financial support for, K-12 public education in the United States are relatively new. For traditionally, the federal government mostly left education to the states and the states delegated the power to local school districts. This resulted in local and state governments having control over local-provided K-12 public education and providing the majority of school district funding.

Only when "national" concerns emerged around critical educational issues, often leading to legal actions—including school (1) racial *segregation*, (2) the effects of school district *poverty* on children learning and lives, or (3) the *failure* of American students to compete and compare favorably with foreign students—particularly the Russian Communists in the 1960s—did the federal government step strongly into the K-12 education policy-making arena.

Title I of the Elementary and Secondary Education Act of 1965 (ESEA), referred to as Every Student Succeeds Act (ESSA), was signed into law in December 2015 by President Obama, and has several programs, including:

Title I: Improving the Academic Achievement of the Disadvantaged

—Part A: Improving the Academic Achievement of the Disadvantaged
—Part B-1: Reading First
—Part C: Migrant and Bilingual Education
—Part D: Institutional Education

ESSA helps the poor, racial desegregation, and national productivity and is an important example of federal interest and involvement in education and its key roles in local schools and districts.

Over the years, Title I has become clearer and more pointed:

I. The purpose of this title is to ensure that all children have a fair, equal, and significant opportunity to obtain a high-quality education and reach, at a minimum, proficiency on challenging State academic achievement standards and state academic assessments. This purpose can be accomplished by

  (1) Ensuring that high-quality academic assessments, accountability systems, teacher preparation and training, curriculum, and instructional materials are aligned with challenging State academic standards so that students, teachers, parents, and administrators can measure progress against common expectations for student academic achievement;

  (2) Meeting the educational needs of low-achieving children in our Nation's highest-poverty schools, limited English proficient children, migratory children, children with disabilities, Indian children, neglected or delinquent children, and young children in need of reading assistance;

  (3) Closing the achievement gap between high- and low-performing children, especially the achievement gaps between minority and nonminority students, and between disadvantaged children and their more advantaged peers;

  (4) Holding schools, local educational agencies, and States accountable for improving the academic achievement of all students, and identifying and turning around low-performing schools that have failed to provide a high-quality education to their students, while providing alternatives to students in such schools to enable the students to receive a high-quality education;

  (5) Distributing and targeting resources sufficiently to make a difference to and schools where needs are greatest;

  (6) Improving and strengthening accountability, teaching, and learning by using State assessment systems designed to ensure that students are meeting challenging State academic achievement and content standards and increasing achievement overall, but especially for the disadvantaged;

  (7) Providing greater decision-making authority and flexibility to schools and teachers in exchange for greater responsibility for student performance;

  (8) Providing children an enriched and accelerated educational program, including the use of school-wide programs or additional services that increase the amount and quality of instructional time;

  (9) Promoting school-wide reform and ensuring the access of children to effective, scientifically based instructional strategies and challenging academic content;

(10) Significantly elevating the quality of instruction by providing staff in participating schools with substantial opportunities for professional development;

(11) Coordinating services under all parts of this title with each other, with other educational services, and, to the extent feasible, with other agencies providing services to youth, children, and families; and

(12) Affording parents substantial and meaningful opportunities to participate in the education of their children.

School principals should come to understand the roles, potential, and limitations of the federal funding and involvement in funding local schools.

For as the U.S. Department of Education explains, "Education is primarily a State and local responsibility in the United States . . . with only about 11 percent Federal funds." And the federal role and influence came late as well, in several areas.

The anti-poverty and civil rights laws of the 1960s and 1970s brought about a dramatic emergence of the department's equal access mission.

- The passage of laws such as Title VI of the Civil Rights Act of 1964, Title IX of the Education Amendments of 1972, and Section 504 of the Rehabilitation Act of 1973 which prohibited discrimination based on race, sex, and disability, respectively, made civil rights enforcement a fundamental and long-lasting focus of the Department of Education.
- In 1965, the ESEA launched a comprehensive set of programs, including the Title I program of federal aid to disadvantaged children to address the problems of poor urban and rural areas. And in that same year, the Higher Education Act authorized assistance for postsecondary education, including financial aid programs for needy college students.

For example, before the mid-1950s, school racial segregation was common nationwide, but especially in the South. So, with the U.S. Supreme Court taking action on May 17, 1954, in the *Brown v. Board of Education*, the federal government worked to "desegregate" America's schools and undue the "separate but equal" approach to education, which meant racial separation. As the Court determined:

After the five cases were heard together by the Court in December 1952, the outcome remained uncertain. The Court ordered the parties to answer a series of questions about the specific intent of the Congressmen and Senators who framed the Fourteenth Amendment to the U.S. Constitution and about the Court's power to dismantle segregation.

Then the Court scheduled another oral argument in December 1953. Wrapping up his presentation to the Court in that second hearing, Thurgood

Marshall emphasized that segregation was rooted in the desire to keep "the people who were formerly in slavery as near to that stage as is possible."

Even with such powerful arguments from Marshall and other LDF attorneys, it took another five months for the newly appointed Chief Justice Earl Warren's behind-the-scenes lobbying to yield a unanimous decision.

Similarly, about two decades later, in the California's courts, families the State for great financial equity sued in the *Serrano v. Priest* (1971) for greater financial equity among school districts, regardless of local real estate property values and wealth equity. As explained (see McDonnell, 2015):

Initiated in 1968 in the Superior Court of Los Angeles County, *Serrano v. Priest* (John Serrano was a parent of one of several Los Angeles public school students; Ivy Baker Priest was the California State Treasurer at the time) set forth three causes of action (quotes from the decision).

California's method of funding public education, because of district-to-district disparities, "fails to meet the requirements of the equal protection clause of the Fourteenth Amendment of the United States Constitution and the California Constitution."

America spent over $550 billion a year on public elementary and secondary education in 2015—and up to $597 billion in 2016—although the distribution of funds, which is often based on local property values and taxes, is unfair and inequitable without the federal government playing a larger role to offset funding disparities. As shown in table 8.1, about $76 billion is federal, while state funding is almost $260 billion, and local contribution is slightly more at nearly $262 billion, with the total almost $600 billion (totaling $597,485,869,000).

And during the so-called War on Poverty, the federal government worked with states and localities to end poverty, in large part, by working to invest in and improve schools.

Thus, this chapter aims to present the key, critical role of—and limitations of—the federal government in working with the fifty states, Washington DC, and the approximately 14,000 local school systems and the public and private school efforts of leadership to tackle major problems, such as literacy, poverty, and future employment for students, while in K-12 schools. This

**Table 8.1.   Spending on Public Schools, K-12, in 2016 School Year**

TOTAL FUNDING OF U.S. PUBLIC EDUCATION in 2016: $597,485,869,000
Federal: $ 75.99 billion (12.7 percent of total)
State: $259.8 billion (43.5 percent of total)
Local: $261.7 billion (43.8 percent of total) wealth and income.
Total: $597,485,869,000 (Approximately $600 billion)

chapter will treat these issues, all around the federal role, responsibility, and impact on local and state K-12 schools and education:

1. **Legal Roles and Actions:** Perhaps the best way to start this analysis is to examine the federal court actions in education that affect local schools and their funding. The *Brown* (1955) decision worked to end racial segregation in U.S. schools and to "integrate" all children into the previously all-white schools. Not easy. As explained, the unanimous court wrote that a quality education was crucial for all children and ruled that it was the state's responsibility to ensure educational equality. The Leadership Conference, "the nation's premier civil & human rights coalition," explains the importance of the *Brown* decision as follows:

   > Today, education is perhaps the most important function of state and local governments. Compulsory school attendance laws and the great expenditures for education both demonstrate our recognition of the importance of education to our democratic society. It is required in the performance of our most basic public responsibilities, even service in the armed forces. It is the very foundation of good citizenship. Today it is a principal instrument in awakening the child to cultural values, in preparing him for later professional training, and in helping him to adjust normally to his environment. In these days, it is doubtful that any child may reasonably be expected to succeed in life if he is denied the opportunity of an education. Such an opportunity, where the state has undertaken to provide it, is a right that must be made available to all on equal terms. (on-line, 2016, Leadership Conference, civilright. on-line).

2. **Federal Efforts and Programs:** Next, we shall present information of federal programs, usually from the U.S. Department of Education, to meet specials needs and difficulties that have triggered national programs such as ESEA and more recently ESSA. Each principal should know and use these programs to help students with needs and disabilities in their schools and districts.

3. **National and State Standards—and Local Needs and Expectations:** Finally, school leaders should become aware of what they need to do to meet expectations and school finances, from all levels: (1) local boards and communities and of course, local superintendents, school board, communities, and even local teacher associations and unions; (2) state departments and other state regulators and regulations; and (3) federal laws, policies, and programs that may benefit children in their schools.

**Driving Funds to Teacher and Students in Classrooms:** School leaders should be aware of how much funding, and "dollars-per-pupil," reach the classrooms in their schools. Cooper and colleagues built a model for tracking dollars to the kids in the classroom. The *resource cost model*, which Chambers recommends, "places paramount importance on measuring productivity and the cost-effectiveness analysis, the economist's stock in trade" (*The Finance Analysis Model: Linking resources for education*—1995, Cooper).

Several states, including Hawaii, South Carolina, and Rhode Island, have adopted another reporting tool that integrates with the existing GAAP accounting systems utilized at the school and district levels. This financial analysis model allows expenditure data to be reported on a school-by-school basis and actually tracks dollars spent on the classroom for "classroom instruction." The reporting program allows policymakers to "explore the equity, efficiency, and effectiveness of spending" (Cooper, Nisonoff, and Speakman, 2001, p. 28) between schools as opposed to school districts.

Moving resources in education into the classroom means better teachers, equipment, materials, books, and opportunities. Hawaii is a case in point, along with South Carolina. We tracked dollars from the state to the child:

**Points of Interest and Importance:** This section of the chapter examines four key areas in which the federal government funding may reach and improve individual schools and how these dollars arrive, should and must be used, and what we can learn from these four examples.

**Case 1: Title 1 and Other ESSA Funding for Poor Children:** The federal government, while highly visible, is usually concentrated on certain key national issues. The main one for more than a half-century was racial and socioeconomic status (SES) equality, so that children regardless of their family's income and location, could and would receive a quality education. The major federal program is ESEA and which just become ESSA.

President Obama signed the ESSA into law on December 10, 2015. ESSA includes provisions that will help to ensure success for students and schools. Below are just a few. The law:

- advances equity by upholding critical protections for America's disadvantaged and high-need students;
- requires—for the first time—that all students in America be taught to high academic standards that will prepare them to succeed in college and careers;
- ensures that vital information is provided to educators, families, students, and communities through annual statewide assessments that measure students' progress toward those high standards;
- helps to support and grow local innovations—including evidence-based and place-based interventions developed by local leaders and educators— consistent with our investing in innovation and promise neighborhoods;
- sustains and expands this administration's historic investments in increasing access to high-quality preschool; and

- maintains an expectation that there will be accountability and action to effect positive change in our lowest-performing schools, where groups of students are not making progress, and where graduation rates are low and over extended. The ESEA was signed into law in 1965 by President Lyndon Baines Johnson, who believed that "full educational opportunity" should be "our first national goal." From its inception, ESEA was a civil rights law to offer quality education to all, regardless of race or background. (Squires and Kubrin, 2005)

ESEA offered new grants to districts serving low-income students, federal grants for textbooks and library books, funding for special education centers, and scholarships for low-income college students. Additionally, the law provided federal grants to state educational agencies to improve the quality of elementary and secondary education.

## NO CHILD LEFT BEHIND (2002): NCLB AND ACCOUNTABILITY

No Child Left Behind (NCLB) Act puts in place measures that exposed achievement gaps among traditionally underserved students and their peers and spurred an important national dialogue on education improvement. This focus on accountability has been critical in ensuring a quality education for all children, yet also revealed challenges in the effective implementation of this goal.

Parents, educators, and elected officials across the country recognized that a strong, updated law was necessary to expand opportunity to all students; to support schools, teachers, and principals; and to strengthen our education system and economy.

In 2012, the Obama administration began granting flexibility to states regarding specific requirements of NCLB in exchange for rigorous and comprehensive state-developed plans designed to close achievement gaps, increase equity, improve the quality of instruction, and increase outcomes for all students.

### What Is Next?

Over the next few weeks, the U.S. Department of Education will work with states and districts to begin implementing the new law.

The NCLB is in the same tradition as ESEA: to help poor children do better in school. As the purpose of the law explains (Klein, 2002):

The No Child Left Behind law—the 2002 update of the Elementary and Secondary Education Act—effectively scaled up the federal role in holding schools accountable for student outcomes.

[It] was the product of a collaboration between civil rights and business groups, as well as both Democrats and Republicans on Capitol Hill and the Bush administration, which sought to advance American competitiveness and close the achievement gap between poor and minority students and their more advantaged peers. Since 2002, it's had an outsized impact on teaching, learning, and school improvement—and become increasingly controversial with educators and the general public. (p. 1)

**Case 2: Special Education Funding for Special Needs-Disabled Children:** Once the Federal Agency worked to handle some of the race and social class (SES) issues in education, to help black and poor children get a good education, the next issue were children with disabilities. First passed in 1975, the federal law, it was recently renewed as Individuals with Disabilities Act (IDEA). Here is a brief history and background on the 1975 law with renewals. As Bishop explains:

The topic of federal funding has been a concern since PL 94–142 (the Education of All Handicapped Children Act, now the Individuals with Disabilities Education Act or IDEA) was passed in 1975. Within this law was a promise of major funding for special education: this legislation mandated that 40 percent of all special education funding would be provided by the federal government. While this level of federal funding is still the expressed goal of many, in reality, this funding has not exceeded 17 percent and typically is closer to 11 to 12 percent. This issue became more of a concern when the recent congressional sequestration went into effect and 9.1 percent was taken from the top of all federal funding, including education for children with disabilities. (Bishop, 2013, pp. 1–2)

**Case 3: Federal Help with Science, Technology, Engineering, and Science (STEM) in Schools:** The Feds have long been concerned about quality math, science, and technology in our schools, for the nation's standing and defense depend on students learning STEM skills, as well as improving manufacturing and life.

For as President Obama explained in March 2015: "[Science] is more than a school subject, or the periodic table, or the properties of waves. It is an approach to the world, a critical way to understand and explore and engage with the world, and then have the capacity to change that world."

President Barack Obama, March 23, 2015, explained:

The United States has developed as a global leader, in large part, through the genius and hard work of its scientists, engineers, and innovators. In a world that's becoming increasingly complex, where success is driven not only by *what* you know, but by what you *can do* with what you know, it's more important than ever for our youth to be equipped with the knowledge and skills to solve tough problems, gather and evaluate evidence, and make sense of information. These are the types of skills that students learn by studying science, technology, engineering, and math—subjects collectively known as STEM.

So as a principle, each of school leaders should follow federal funding for STEM, as it comes down the pipe, or the computer.

**Case 4: Special Federal Funding for Schools:** The federal role—and financial support—for K-12 public education in the United States are both fairly new and very complex. For previously, the Feds mostly left education to each of the states and local school districts, which meant that we had mainly local and state funding and control of education. Only when "national" concerns emerged around critical issues—including school racial segregation, the effects of school district poverty, and/or the failure of American students to compete with foreign kids, particularly the Russian Communists in the 1960s in the sciences—did the federal government (i.e., the president, Congress and U.S. Department of Education) step into K-12 educational policymaking, nationwide with important effects on school finance.

Title I of ESEA for the poor, racial desegregation for black kids and Latinos/as, and national productivity are three important examples of the federal interest in education, and their key roles in local schools and districts. Principals should come to understand the roles, potential, and limitations of the federal involvement in funding local schools. For as the U.S. Department of Education explains, "Education is primarily a State and local responsibility in the United States . . ." with only about 11 percent Federal funds" and the role and influence came late as well, in several areas.

The anti-poverty and civil rights laws of the 1960s and 1970s brought about a dramatic emergence of the department's equal access mission.

- The passage of laws such as Title VI of the Civil Rights Act of 1964, Title IX of the Education Amendments of 1972, and Section 504 of the Rehabilitation Act of 1973 which prohibited discrimination based on race, sex, and disability, respectively, made civil rights enforcement a fundamental and long-lasting focus of the Department of Education.
- In 1965, the ESEA launched a comprehensive set of programs, including the Title I program of federal aid to disadvantaged children to address the problems of poor urban and rural areas. And in that same year, the Higher Education Act authorized assistance for postsecondary education, including financial aid programs for needy college students.
- For example, before the mid-1950s, school racial segregation was common in the South and other areas of the nation. So, with the U.S. Supreme

Court taking action on May 17, 1954, in the *Brown v. Board of Education*, the federal government worked to "desegregated" America's schools. Similarly, about two decades later, California's courts sued in the *Serrano v. Priest* (1971) for greater financial equity among school districts, regardless of local real property values and wealth equity. As explained:

Initiated in 1968 in the Superior Court of Los Angeles County, *Serrano v. Priest* (John Serrano was a parent of one of several Los Angeles public school students; Ivy Baker Priest was the California State Treasurer at the time) set forth three causes of action (quotes from the decision).

California's method of funding public education, because of district-to-district disparities, "fails to meet the requirements of the equal protection clause of the Fourteenth Amendment of the United States Constitution and the California Constitution."

America spent over $550 billion a year on public elementary and secondary education in 2015—and up to $597 billion in 2016—although the distribution of funds is often based on local property and is often not fair or equitable.

## SPENDING ON PUBLIC SCHOOLS, K-12, IN 2016 SCHOOL YEAR

TOTAL FUNDING OF U.S. PUBLIC EDUCATION in 2016: $597,485, 869,000
Federal: $75.99 billion (12.7 percent of total)
State: $259.8 billion (43.5 percent of total)
Local: $261.7 billion (43.8 percent of total) wealth and income.

And during the so-called War on Poverty, the federal government worked with states and localities to end poverty, in large part, by improving U.S school.

Thus, this chapter aims to present the key, critical role of the federal government in working with the fifty states, Washington, DC, and the approximately 14,000 local school systems and the public and private school leadership to tackle major problems, such as literacy, poverty, and future employment for students, while in K-12 schools.

1. **Legal Role and Actions:** Perhaps the best way to start is to examine the federal court actions in education that affect local schools and their funding.
2. **Federal Efforts and Programs:** Next, we shall present information of federal programs, usually from the U.S. Department of Education, to meet

specials needs and difficulties that have triggered national programs such as ESEA and recently ESSA. Each principal should know and use these programs to help students with needs and disabilities in their schools and districts.

3. **National and State Standards—and Local Needs and Expectations:** Finally, school leaders should become aware of what they need to do to meet expectations and school finances, from all levels: (1) local boards and communities and of course, local superintendents, school board, communities, and even local teacher associations and unions; (2) state departments and other state regulators and regulations; and (3) federal laws, policies, and programs that may benefit children in their schools.

## SPECIAL SPENDING FOR CHILDREN WITH SPECIAL NEEDS

The IDEA is the chief legislative and mandated program of and service driver for special education. However, IDEA has been underfunded since its inception in 1975. Although President Obama promised full funding of IDEA, he has not sought or produced full funding as yet. The President's FY-2017 budget funds IDEA at FY-2016 levels of only 16 percent of the full cost of all IDEA special education-mandated programs and services.

The underfunding of IDEA at only 16 percent is less than half of the federal government's original 40 percent limit on funding students with educational and physiological disabilities. Moreover, the federal government promised to pay only 40 percent of the national average per special education pupil expenditure penalizing districts with higher-than- average per- pupil special education expenditures. The highest funding level provided by the federal government for funding IDEA's mandated programs and services was 18 percent in 2005. This means that President Obama's proposed funding level for FY2017 is below that of more than a decade ago under President Bush.

Funding IDEA at only 16 percent means that 84 percent must be paid for by public school districts themselves, nation-wide, because the IDEA's programs and services are mandated. These programs and services require that any funding deficit be paid for by the public school districts themselves. Therefore, under-funding IDEA requires districts to make up for the dollar shortfall by cutting non-mandate-protected programs and services.

Hence, the underfunding of IDEA is one of the most powerful drivers of public school district budget cuts nationwide. Moreover, the chronic underfunding of IDEA and the budget cuts it fosters often pit regular and special education parents, students, and teachers against one another in a battle for scarce financial, material, and human educational resources.

**Question**: Should not the federal government be required to pay 100 percent of its special education mandates?

**Answer:** Special education expenses are one of the fastest growing financial challenges confronting school districts nationwide and particularly in New Jersey. School districts throughout New Jersey pay not only all of the general expense for their special education students but also the majority of the "excess cost" of special education. Excess cost is defined as the per- pupil cost of special education that exceeds the regular student cost.

Declining state and federal aid not only has increased the proportion of property taxes used to fund schools but has also heightened the pressure to find necessary resources perhaps by reducing programs and services for regular education students in order to fund mandate-protected programs and services such as special education.

Special education costs are driven primarily by expensive out-of-district placements; by mandated preschool programs, including intensive services for autistic students; by lower special education student-to-staff ratios; and by parents suing school districts to obtain private school placements for their children. The legal fees for such lawsuits account for another escalating expense for schools.

In addition, if a school district loses in a New Jersey Administrative Court, the district not only has to pay for the judgment costs but also has to pay all of the plaintiff's legal costs regardless of the length of the trial. It seems as if holding New Jersey school districts harmless from such law suits would be another way to enable school districts to allocate more of their scarce resources to instruction.

Many districts find that out-of-district placements can consume as much as 50 percent of the special education budget. The students placed in out-of-district schools tend to be the most expensive because they are usually the ones most in need of special educational programs and services. Depending on the student's disability, the annual cost of sending a student to an out-of-district private school can range from roughly $60,000 to over $250,000— especially for the most educationally and physically challenged students.

The federal government forces its traditional public schools to pay for an ever-increasing proportion of special education costs by underfunding IDEA mandates, forcing districts to increase local property taxes and identify funds to offset the shortfall through means that adversely impact the regular education budget. Underfunded IDEA mandates can result in much larger class sizes as school districts are forced to consider reducing regular education teachers and aides. Larger class sizes often lead to lower test scores that make it more difficult for students, schools, and districts to achieve academic progress and control costs.

Unless public school districts, nationwide, not only wish to avoid IDEA-driven budget cuts to offset IDEA's underfunding and a downward spiral in the quality of education stemming from IDEA's underfunding but also wish for continued higher property taxes, then the districts nationwide should band together and demand that the federal government fund IDEA 100 percent, and therefore, pay for all of the costs of IDEA's mandated programs and services.

Moreover, fully funding IDEA would prevent the budget cuts it currently fosters. Stopping IDEA-driven budget cuts would end the conflict among regular and special education parents, students, and teachers over scarce financial, material, and human educational resources, and put the focus on working together to provide a quality education for all.

## POINTS OF INTEREST AND IMPORTANCE

This section of the chapter examines four key areas in which the federal government's funding may reach and improve individual schools and their students. And we examine just how these dollars arrive, how these should and must be used to improve schools and their students' learning—and what we can learn from these four cases (Cooper and Speakman, 1997).

### Special Federal Funding for High Education in the United States

*The Land Grant College Act and GI Bill*

In the history of the United States, two federal funding programs stand out: In 1865, Congress passed the Land Grant College Act, which distributed thousands of acres of federal land to the states to open "agricultural and technical colleges" ("ag-tech"). Some states sold the former federal land and made use of the funds to open and build new ag-tech colleges all across the country; other states opened colleges on the land grant acres. Virtually every state now has important ag-tech colleges for teaching agriculture and engineering. New York has Cornell that is partially public land grant and part private, with most of the professional and technical schools remaining public, and the undergraduate colleges being private.

The other important federal program was the GI Bill (1944), passed at the end of World War II to educate the millions of men and women who had sacrificed their education and sometimes their lives—and served in the military. Millions have financed their higher education using funds from the GI Bill. President Roosevelt signed the law into action:

> On June 22, 1944, President Franklin D. Roosevelt signed the Servicemen's Readjustment Act, better known as the G.I. Bill. Fearing the consequences of millions of veterans returning from war to scarce employment and housing

opportunities, Roosevelt passed the legislation to offer unemployment compensation, home and business loans and college tuition support.

Thus, when the federal government thinks big, the results are often commensurately big; and the bigger the problem, the bigger the solution at the national level. The federal government can create its own program in education, or fund the local and states efforts. Either way, every level can benefit. And the bill was called the GI Bill of Rights:

> The initials "GI" originally stood for anything of "government issue." Eventually, they came to designate an enlisted soldier in the U. S. armed forces. In 1944 Congress passed the Servicemen's Readjustment Act, the so-called GI Bill of Rights, which provided government aid (a) for veterans' hospitals and vocational rehabilitation; (b) for the purchase by veterans of houses, farms, and businesses; and (c) for four years of college education for veterans. Later, the act extended to veterans of the Korean War. The Readjustment Benefits Act of 1966 gave similar rights to all veterans of service in the U. S. armed forces, whether during wartime or peacetime. Subsequent acts provided for additional benefits. With the abolition of the draft in 1973, benefits were tied to length of service. (Berman, 2015, p. 1)

Therefore, the federal government and its policies are remote from most American school children, their schools, teachers, and families. But the federal government plays an important role, setting legal policies and precedents, and often in a position to influence the schools by offering advice, funding, and legal remedies. Or as one agency explained, During the past half century, federal education policy has played an increasingly critical role in determining what happens in American classrooms—and ultimately in the minds and hearts of American students.

Thus, administrators in our schools need to be aware, keep pace, and live by the federal requirement, as best they can, as the Southern Education Research Board (2015) explains:

> As a result, despite federal mandates, state interventions and system expenditures of millions of dollars earmarked for reform, many school districts serving high-needs students have a substantial percentage of schools not meeting Adequate Yearly Progress (AYP) goals under the federal *No Child Left Behind Act*. (p. 20)

## REFERENCES

Berman, E. (June 22, 2015). "How the G.I. Bill Changed the Face of Higher Education in America," *Life Education. TIME*. On-line: Time.com.

Bishop, N. (August 21, 2013). "What Do Federal Budget Cuts Really Mean for Public School Special Education Programs?" *Special Education Guide*. Available at http://www.specialeducationguide.com/blog/what-do-federal-budget-cuts-really-mean-for-public-school-special-education-programs/.

Cooper, B. S., Nisonoff, P. H., & Speakman, S. T. (2001). Advanced budget technology in education: The future is now. *School Business Affairs*, *67*(2), pp. 27–32.

Cooper, B. S., & Randall, E. V. (1998). From transactional to transformational accounting. *School Business Affairs*, *64*(4), pp. 4–16.

Cooper, B. S., & Speakman, S. T. (1997). The three R's of education finance reform: Re-thinking, re-tooling, and re-evaluating school-site information. *Journal of Education Finance*, *22*(4), pp. 337–67.

Klein, A. (2002). *No Child Left Behind: An overview*. Available at http://www.edweek.org/ew/section/multimedia/no-child-left-behind-overview-definition-summary.html.

McDonnell, L. M. (2005). No Child Left Behind and the federal role in education: Evolution or revolution? *Peabody Journal of Education*, *80*(2), pp. 19–38.

Southern Education Research Board. (2012). *Federal education policy and the states, 1945–2009: A brief synopsis*. Albany, NY: The New York State Department of Education.

*Chapter 9*

# Budgeting and Managing
# for Local Revenues

## Stephen Coffin and Bruce S. Cooper

### INTRODUCTION

One of the defining characteristics of American public schools is their importance, "local control" and, yes, funding. Local dollars coming from property taxes provide the majority of funding for the majority of districts nationwide. While state and federal governments contribute additional, significant funding, in most states—Hawaii is an exception with no local districts—are locally funded and managed. This localism means that the community and the school boards, superintendents, and principals have a strong voice in the control and management of our local public schools. As the National School Boards Association explained,

> The most important responsibility of school boards is to work with their communities to improve student achievement in their local public schools. School boards derive their power and authority from the state. In compliance with state and federal laws, school boards establish policies and regulations by which their local schools are governed.—See more (https://www.nsba.org/about-us/frequently-asked-questions#sthash. 9KQci Uyc.dpuf, 2001)

Within the fifty states, as explained by the 2012 Census of Governments, the U. S. Census Bureau enumerated the following numbers of school systems in the United States: 13,506 school district governments in the fifty states. Thus, we shall explore and explain the local nature, control, and funding of American public (and some private) schools, including the advantages and disadvantages of local funding—and control—of our schools.

## Advantages of Local Control and Funding

Both the local control and funding of public schools have certain major advantages. First, teachers, principals, and parents have a greater voice in local education, with less statewide and national influence. After all, school boards are basic, local *democratic institutions that* represent their educators, families, and stakeholders of their local communities. The American Legislature Exchange Council explains the role of local school boards as follows:

> The Innovation Schools and School Districts Act creates a mechanism for schools, groups of schools, and districts to adopt plans that try new ways of delivering instruction and/or allocating resources. It creates a new classification of school districts, "Districts of Innovation," that have one or more schools implementing these plans. Districts of innovation are provided a greater degree of autonomy and can waive some statutory requirements. (The Innovation Schools and School Districts Act, 2015, p. 1).

Second, teachers can form local spokes groups for their schools and classrooms, because most states have laws that allow local "collective bargaining" and union activity. This "voice" is particularly important in the larger, urban districts where teachers need someone to speak for their needs in the classroom in teaching their subjects and in receiving decent pay and benefits (e.g., health care, tenure, benefits, and pensions). While most states allow a collective voice through unionization and collective bargaining, some still do not. While teachers do not "speak" with one union voice, as the United Federation of Teachers and the larger National Education Association (NEA) were not able to agree to merge (see Cooper, 1998), the two unions speak up when teachers need them (Fusarelli and Cooper, 1999); but a merger was rejected by the NEA in New Orleans in 1998.

For example, the NEA explained its role and position on local school polities and programs, as follows:

> That effort received a big boost last week in Washington, DC, when the country's largest union, the National Education Association (NEA), voted at its national convention to support the Portland resolution and to encourage state and local affiliates to create and promote climate literacy resolutions in their own communities, using the Portland resolution as a model. The NEA has close to 3 million members, and its convention is dubbed "the world's largest deliberative assembly," with 7,000 delegates. (Bigalow, 2016)

Even the 2016 presidential election candidates spoke and argued over local education and funding; the NEA supported the Democratic candidate, Hillary R. Clinton, who explained her relationship with teachers:

> The NEA enthusiastically responded to Hillary's bridge building, and it heard her promise to do what teachers want the most from officeholders. We want to

be partners. We want to be re-invited by a president to our "seat at the table." We want a president—not just a presidential candidate—who says and believes, "I have this old-fashioned idea that when we are making decisions about education, we actually should listen to our educators." (Thompson, 2016, p. 2)

And Donald J. Trump had his own view of school spending, as he explained just before his presidential campaign (White, 2016, pp. 22–23).

### *We spend more per student than any other nation—*

Education spending: "People are tired of spending more money on education than any nation in the world per capita."

Local control of education: "Education has to be local."

American education in an international context: "We're 26th in the world. 25 countries are better than us at education. And some of them are like third world countries. But we're becoming a third world country."

## Equity among School Districts' Spending on Education

A second critical issue involving local control and funding of our public schools is the lack of district spending equity, often based on differences in local residential and business property wealth, among districts in the same state. Much like the desegregation efforts in the 1950s following the *Brown v. Board of Education of Topeka, Kansas* (1955), school-funding inequalities court cases began about seventeen years later, with the California case, *Serrano v. Priest* (California Supreme Court: *Serrano v. Priest*, 5 Cal.3d 584 (1971)).

The issue is that since local "property values" differ, and thus poorer school districts have problems trying to raise sufficient funds for their schools, they turn to the state for funding. As the case came to explain:

Initiated in 1968 in the Superior Court of Los Angeles County, *Serrano v. Priest* (John Serrano was a parent of one of several Los Angeles public school students; Ivy Baker Priest was the California State Treasurer at the time) set forth three causes of action (quotes from the decision).

California's method of funding public education, because of district-to-district disparities, "fails to meet the requirements of the equal protection clause of the Fourteenth Amendment of the United States Constitution and the California Constitution."

"[As] a direct result of the financing scheme they are required to pay a higher tax rate than [taxpayers] in many other school districts in order to obtain for their children the same or lesser educational opportunities afforded children in those other districts."

"[That] an actual controversy has arisen and now exists between the parties as to the validity and constitutionality of the financing scheme under the

Fourteenth Amendment of the United States Constitution and under the California Constitution."

The Court agreed with the plaintiffs, largely on equal-protection grounds, and returned the case to the trial court for further proceedings.

In the end, the *Serrano* decision in California—and similar cases in other states—ruled that local districts are often fiscally inequitable based on funding, since local property wealth varies greatly from district to district and that the state has a legal responsibility in many states to help equalize local spending by subsidizing local funding. As one explanation of the effects of *Serrano* in California and in similar cases in other states:

> After Serrano I, the Legislature enacted SB90, which established a "squeeze formula" to begin a leveling of recurring school-district income based on the average daily attendance revenue limit. The Superior Court in *Serrano* ruled in 1974 that, although SB90 was a step in the right direction, "wealth-related disparities" were still impermissible. Serrano II affirmed the trial court's judgment, giving the state six years to bring the system into compliance. (See more at: http://corporate.findlaw.com/law-library/separate-and-unequal-serrano-played-an-important-role-in.html#sthash.6Of9oveN.dpuf, 1975.)

And the courts moved to create greater equity and equality of per-pupil spending for districts with poor property wealth and thus lower property tax income for schools. As the courts determined,

> Thus, in 1968–69, the Baldwin Park School District spent $577.49 to educate each of its pupils, while Pasadena spent $840.19 and Beverly Hills spent $1,231.72. This "economic chasm" between various districts with respect to tax base and expenditures meant "poorer" districts had to tax themselves at much higher rates to match the expenditures of wealthier districts, if this was even possible.
>
> As the Supreme Court put it, "affluent districts can have their cake and eat it too; they can provide a high quality education for their children while paying lower taxes. Poor districts, by contrast, have no cake at all." (1979)

Equity is the major issue across districts in the state, based on property wealth and taxation. As was shown in the *Serrano* case in California and later in other states, the issue remains important as follows:

> The statistics recited in Serrano I were provocative. Recurring public-school funds came primarily from local district taxes on real property (55.7 percent) and State School Fund aid (35.5 percent). The Legislature authorized each county to levy taxes on real property within a school district at a rate needed to meet the district's annual education budget. (See more at: http://corporate.

findlaw.com/law-library/separate-and-unequal-serrano-played-an-important-role-in.html#sthash.6Of9oveN.dpuf, 1981).

## How Many Dollars Are Reaching Students in the Classroom?

The next issue gets even closer to teachers and their students in the class: *How much money in each district reaches the child in the classroom?* (Cooper and Randall, 1998). In 1973, Bruce S. Cooper and Sheree T. Speakman at Coopers & Lybrand built a model called Financial Analysis Model (FAM) or *In$ite* for tracking dollars from the central office to the school to the classroom.

FAM was developed for NYC Mayor Rudy Giuliani since NYC spent millions on education but was having trouble producing well-educated, high-testing students. As one description explains,

This proposal's signatories call on policymakers to transform the school funding system in service of meeting our high ambitions for student learning. We envision a transparent system in which:

- Funding from all levels follows every student to whichever public school he or she attends;
- The amount varies according to the student's needs;
- Funding arrives at schools a *real dollars* that can be spent flexibly, with accountability gauged *results* rather than inputs, programs, or activities. Cooper, Bruce S., & Speakman, Sheree T. (1997)

The FAM is being used by districts across the country to increase and improve the use of funding, by driving the resources to the actual teachers in the actual classrooms, where the students are taught and are learning. If an over amount of resources are spent on "overhead," administration, and other nonpedagogical purposes, the kids and their teachers can suffer. Poverty begins at home and carries over to the classroom.

Budgeting and budget analysis are important activities and points of analysis. William Hartman (1999) has dissected and analyzed models of budgeting that can help each school leader to improve the results and uses of budgeting and funding.

## TYPES OF OPERATING BUDGETS

1. **Line-item Budgeting:** Mundt, Olsen, and Steinberg (1982) define line item, or "traditional," budgeting as "a technique in which line items, or objects of expenditures—e.g., personnel, supplies, contractual services,

and capital outlays—are the focus of analysis, authorization, and control" (p. 36). While helpful in tracking costs, line-item budgeting is virtually useless for planning or management, because the functions of the expenditures are not explained and the particular need, school site, and type of students being served are lost in spending aggregated by "line." Thus, teachers' salaries, for example, are a budget line item; but which teachers, at which schools, teaching which types of students (e.g., bilingual special needs, ELL, English as a Second Language) is not explained.

2. **Function/Object Budgeting:** Most districts use function/object budgeting, because it organizes spending around the basic functions of the system, such as instruction, student support, operations, administration, and transportation. In addition, functions are subdivided (e.g., into elementary instruction, middle-school operations, high-school operations), while the object being purchased (e.g., elementary textbooks, middle-school windows, high-school cleaning equipment) is also specified. Personnel services or salaries and benefits may be handled by function, that is, for instructional, support, or plant maintenance staff, for example.

Although these broad categories, objects, and processes are generally the same for education budgeting across the country, a strategic attempt has also been made to determine the most effective and efficient uses of resources. These efforts have led to such innovations as zero-based, program-planning, and site-based budgeting, which attempt to be more mission-driven and constituent-friendly than traditional types of budgeting in education.

3. **Zero-based Budgeting:** Popular in the 1950s and 1960s, zero-based budgeting (ZBB) began with the assumption that the school system starts out yearly with a "clean slate" or at zero, with no contents. Thus, each function, program, and agency has to justify its expenditures annually, relating all costs to system goals and objectives to avoid habitual spending.

Thus, budgets are built from the ground or from "zero" up. Because many costs, such as tenured teachers' salaries and benefits, are "fixed" across annual budgets, and because the programs are so complex, ZBB becomes more an exercise than a practical reality. As Hartman (1999) explains, "ZBB . . . forces comparisons of and choices among programs and activities that are often difficult to compare adequately" (p. 49). In addition, most programs are not "up for grabs" on an annual basis, since, for example, schools cannot eliminate their elementary school classes, making such a requirement difficult to justify.

ZBB is not weak in challenging past year but strong because it does not just carryover all of prior year when programs or service levels may have changed, but it also does not carryover past year's forecasts and assumptions. ZBB is designed to avoid carrying over priorities and plans as reflected in the budget. ZBB, while most helpful and sound, requires a great deal of time by all key stakeholders. ZBB combined with site-based budgeting (SBB) is perhaps the best approach. SBB tailors the budget more to the unique needs of each school and schools vary by student needs within districts.

4. **Program-Planning-Budgeting Systems:** Used by the U.S. Defense Department during the Vietnam War, Program-planning-budgeting systems (PPBS) seek greater efficiency by attaching spending to particular programs (e.g., the development of a new multipurpose fighter jet aircraft that might be used jointly by the Army, Navy, and Air Force—thus saving costs, but failing, in fact, to meet the needs of any of the armed services very well).

   While rarely used in education, PPBS would require school districts to spell out their mission and goals, lay out alternatives to reach these objectives, attribute costs to each choice, analyze the costs, select the best option, and then build the budget around this outcome, and finally feed data back to adjust the costs to the results. While this method sounds ideal, it often becomes overly complex, and the programs so numerous, that school districts and states cannot readily sustain this approach.

5. **Site-based (School-site) Budgeting:** SBB is concerned with who will do the budgeting and where in the organizational hierarchy the decisions will be made. In attempts to bring the budgeting process closer to "end-users"—the teachers, parents, and school administrators—SBB encourages, if not requires, decision makers in each school to examine their programs and to set their budgets to meet their particular needs as part of the process of shared decision-making.

Allan Odden et al. (2012) explain that school reforms may require greater decentralization, a step "in which teams of individuals who actually provide the services are given decision-making authority and held accountable for results" (p. 5). Under SBB, districts must determine who will serve on SBB committees; which decisions and resources are devolved to schools—and using what formulas; how much autonomy is granted to spend for local school needs; exactly how to analyze the budget at each school; and what training and support are needed to make SBB work effectively.

In practice, school districts or divisions thereof will utilize variations of many, if not all, of the above methods in compiling their budgets. For example, a school principal may require teachers to justify their individual budget requests (ZBB) in the development of a school (SBB) budget. A component of the district's budget may include a proposal for a new educational program, including all anticipated expenditures, revenues, and cost savings (PPBS). The entire district budget may be compiled onto a state-mandated format that requires line items to be categorized by fund, function, program, and object (function/object budgeting).

Outcome-focused budgeting is positive: it relates to outcomes which after all are what education is all about; but regarded as too time-consuming and complex (few seem to ever wish to agree on outcomes let alone put them in writing so they can be held accountable to them!) Once the FY begins, the budget is transformed from a financial plan into the initial baseline data for a working, dynamic financial accounting system.

### How Effective Is the Use of Funding, Measured "How?"

The final step, therefore, is to connect money to results, outcomes, and student improvements in academic performance. Teachers have no control over whom they teacher and what level the students are operating at when they enter their classrooms in the autumn or spring. Good financial analysis should somehow relate "bucks to outcomes," which is difficult in education.

### CONCLUSION

The principal is the "CEO" for his or her school; therefore, he or she should know every room, field, closet, hallway, and bathroom; where the supplies and materials are stored; where the teachers are assigned and why they are assigned as they are; his or her school community; and most of all, what are the needs and priorities of the school. However, per-pupil costs can vary by class such as high school science (e.g., chemistry labs) can be more expensive than English literature.

Similarly, per-pupil costs can be higher in elementary grades that use manipulatives than in ones that do not; also computer-oriented classes can have higher per-pupil costs for technology-related expenditures. Purchase orders and close monitoring of purchasing is essential to sound budgeting because much waste and corruption centers of purchasing: intentional over paying per unit amounts or receiving less quantity or lower quality but same quantity of items purchased per purchase order. Business administrators and principals must be aware of how mistakes, even innocent mistakes, can occur.

Principal leadership is essential to sound budgeting, especially when using SBB, indicating principals should have training and instruction in budgeting and school finance to succeed in managing budgets and their schools' operations. Perhaps one way to reflect on the budget's importance is to consider the following budget impact on the classroom common parlance metric: if it (e.g., meaning key programs, services, technology, materials, furniture, supplies, etc.) is not in your budget (i.e., for classroom, school, or district), then it would not be in your classroom. This is an important guiding principle to keep in mind when budgeting for schools.

# REFERENCES

Bigalow, W. (2016). "The Nation's Largest Teachers Union Endorses Teaching 'Climate Justice.'" *Huntington Post.*

Cooper, B. S. (1998). Merging the teachers unions: Opportunity amid complexity. "Commentary". *Education Week.* March 11, 1998, pp. 52, 34.

Cooper, B. S. (March 11, 1998). "Merging the Teachers' Unions." *Education Week Commentary,* March 11, 1998, pp. 30–32.

Cooper, B. S. (1999). "Merging the AFT and the NEA." *Annual Developments in Education.* New York: Gale Publishing.

Cooper, B. S., & Liotta, M. (November 2001). Urban teachers unions face their future: The dilemmas of organizational maturity. *Education and Urban Society, 31*(1), pp. 101–18.

Cooper, B. S., & Speakman, S. T. (1997). "The Three R's of Education Finance Reform: Re-Thinking, Re-Tooling, and Re-Evaluating School-Site Information. *Journal of Education Finance, 22*(4), pp. 337–367.

Cooper, B. S., & Speakman, S. T. (2001). "Advanced Budgeting Technology in Education: The Future is Now," School Business Affairs. February 2001.

Fusarelli, L. D., & Cooper, B. S. (1999). Why the NEA and AFT sought to merge— and failed. *School Business Affairs, 65*(4), pp. 33–38.

Hartman, W. T. (1999). *School district budgeting.* Reston, VA: Association of School Business Officials International.

Mundt, B., Olsen, R., & Steinberg, H. J. (1982). *Accounting public school budgeting and auditing, budgeting, accounting, auditing, future trends, managing public resources.* New York: Peat Marwick International.

National School Boards Association. Available at https://www.nsba.org/about-us/frequently-asked-questions#sthash. 9KQci Uyc.dpuf.

Odden, A. R., & Picus, L. O. (2014). *School finance: A policy perspective* (5th ed.). New York: McGraw Hill.

Odden, A., & Picus, L. O. (2015). *2015 Wyoming recalibration report.* Prepared for the Wyoming Select Committee on School Finance Recalibration. North Hollywood, CA: Lawrence O. Picus and Associates. Available at http://picusodden.com/wp-content/uploads/2013/09/Picus-Odden-Nov-2015-WY-Recalib-Report.pdf.

Thompson, John. (July 8, 2016). "Hillary and the Education History That Teachers Can't Forget." 07/08/2016 09:29 am ET | p. 2.

White, B. (2016). Fordham Institute, EduWatch.

*Section III*

# CHANGES AND EFFECTIVENESS NOW AND IN THE FUTURE

This final section of the book examines alternative funding approaches and policies for schools in the United States, including privatization, vouchers and charter school programs, and even homeschooling—and the operation and effectiveness of these school-site financial programs. For we believe that local school leaders should be aware of what is going on the "private education sector," both (1) to learn and understand these programs and (2) to see the relationship between public and private education locally, as a means of improving all schooling and funding and helping all children in the United States.

For school funds, that is, *coins*, have two sides: the public tax side and the private, individual, and sometimes religiously focused funding side. These two sides of the same coin are often critical for school leaders of all schools to understand.

And does privatization sometimes break some problems of the "monopolies" of the local public schools? Do these programs work to create competition? And thus, can they function to improve teaching and student outcomes for all children in both the public and private sectors of education?

*Chapter 10*

# Privatization, Vouchers, and Tuition Tax Credits

## *A More Public View*

### Stephen Coffin and Bruce S. Cooper

Education is both a vital public community service and a private personal concern, including critical programs and systems of policies, since both parents and their children are seeking a quality, appropriate education—for members of their families. Society, too, seeks to support a good education for children, regardless of their family's income, race, religious beliefs, and/or the location of their schools.

Hence, education leaders—at both the school building and district levels— should understand the various public government sources, as well as the concept of "privatization" and the *private education sector*, including its funding, organization, and control. For a quality K-12 education for all youngsters is essential, and includes a wide range of school options that are public, private, religious, independent, and family based such as "homeschooling" (see Cooper, 2005; Cooper and Spielhagen, 2016). Six states have recently expanded family choice, including private schools, as shown in figure 10.1 below.

As reported on May 1, 2015: "As it brought nature to abundant life, April brought hope to children, with legislatures in six states approving measures to expand the rights of parents to choose their child's school."

Lawmakers in Arizona, Arkansas, Mississippi, Montana, Nevada, and Tennessee (see figure 10.1) thrust the school choice movement into warp drive with an impressive mix of new programs, including education savings accounts, vouchers, tax credits, and tax-credit scholarships. Except for Montana, perhaps, all the bills have been, or likely will soon be, signed into law.

These nonpublic schools and programs now involve a total of about 6.5 million school children; and thus it is important that school leaders and policymakers understand their funding and organization—public and private, religious, and independent—for about 9 percent of students in the United States now attend other-than-public schools. Private (nonpublic) education

**Figure 10.1.  States Passing School Choice Laws Recently**

is here for a long time—and growing—and should be understood by public school leaders at the district and building levels as a major purpose of this book on school-site financial leadership.

This chapter explores and explains different approaches to funding non-public schools, both religious and nonsectarian. We see that the public system—and its long monopolistic funding—is being challenged by nonpublic and religious funding policies and programs—and schools. Thus, under privatization, funds can go to families—and their children—and *then to the school or program of their choice.*

Richer and more religious families (e.g., Catholic, Protestant, Jewish, and now Muslim) have often funded their own children's education in the private sector; now the governments at the state and federal levels are more often allowing parents-families with all incomes to go "private" and "buy" their education of choice.

Thus, this chapter is organized to help school leaders and teachers to understand and respond to the forces of privatization, and what might be required to work with and even be controlled by them. These choices are complex—but interesting—giving educational leaders a sense of the forces of "markets and choice in education," sometimes replacing the near "monopoly" of public education in the United States, and how their schools are now "competing" with other programs, schools, and homeschooling options. These options—or "new education mixes"—include the following policies and programs: vouchers, charter schools, homeschools, and private schools.

## THE RISE AND DROP OF AMERICAN CATHOLIC
## SCHOOLS AND ENROLLMENTS

Private education in the United States, in the past, often meant *Catholic parochial* (or parish) and diocesan K-12 schools. A brief history: when Catholic immigrants from Ireland, Italy, Eastern Europe, and other countries came to the United States and placed their children in the local public schools in the nineteenth century, many found the public schools too "Protestant," as classes were reading the St James Bible and praying the Lord's Prayer. When parents complained to their local Catholic Church priests and bishops, these leaders began to open their own Catholic parish schools, often run by sisters (nuns).

Costs were low since parish churches gave a portion of each Sunday collections ("passing the plate") to their local schools; and these schools were comfortable places for recent Catholic immigrants. These private schools grew and expanded, to include Catholic high schools, often run by religious orders. And many teenage Catholic children went from the local parish school to the regional diocesan Catholic high schools.

By 1965—the peak year for Catholic K-12 education in the United States—over 5.66 million American children were enrolled in some 18,000 Catholic schools across the United States, and the Catholic schools became a model for other religious schools run by groups such as Lutherans, Seventh Day Adventists, Jews, Evangelical Protestants, Muslims, and nonsectarian groups like Montessori and independent school organizations (affiliates of the National Association of Independent Schools [NAIS]). But sadly, as Arianna Prothero (2014) found more recently:

> From 2004 to 2014, U.S. Catholic school enrollment dropped by 43 percent, to fewer than 2 million [1.7 million] students, compared with 5.66 million at the pinnacle of such enrollment in the 1960s [1965], according to data compiled by the National Catholic Educational Association, based in Arlington, Va. The decline is even more pronounced in urban areas, where a combination of changing demographics, rising tuition costs, and increased competition from free, public charter schools, are exacting its toll on inner-city Catholic schools. (p. 55)

The private sector was well developed until the 1970s—and later, when the Catholic schools began to close—falling to only about 1.7 million kids in less than 7,000 schools in 2011. Cooper has just published a chapter—in a book edited by Gerald Cattaro and Charles Russo (2015)—on the decline of Catholic nonpublic schools and the increase in many other types of private schools (see Cooper, 2015, chapter in a book, *Gravissimum Educationis*, remembering the fiftieth anniversary of Vatican II (Cattaro and Russo, 2015). By now, we have about as many nonpublic schools and enrollments as the peak in 1965; but Catholic schools are only about 35 percent of the national private school total (Cooper and Zhu, 2016).

## State Funding of Vouchers or Tuition Tax Credits

The public funding of students' education—through a grant to their parents—is called a "voucher," whereby public dollars "follow the children" to the "schools of their choice," with parent as decision makers and kids as beneficiaries at a school of their chosen school. A number of states now support voucher programs, with more coming every year. Vouchers can empower the parents and children to become key decision makers, with the public funding following the children to their schools of choice. Vouchers have been around for a long time, as governments have long given resources to parents to educate their certain children.

A statewide voucher or tuition tax credit scholarship program can provide a tuition grant of $10,000 annually to any student attending a failing local public school or district with failing schools. These vouchers can be applied to any private, religious, or independent school that lacks educational quality or equity, does not provide an equal educational opportunity for all students, and diverts scare funds from traditional public school (TPS) districts. Asymmetric information would adversely affect voucher users. Not all students have equal knowledge of or access to desirable private religious or independent schools.

Private religious or independent schools may not be equitably available within a twenty-mile radius. Tax credits disproportionately benefit the affluent and could result in the public subsidizing the voucher program. The voucher program provides an unequal opportunity for students to attend a private or religious school potentially producing a higher quality education for some students. Moreover, state subsidies of religious schools may violate the constitutional separation of church and state.

The voucher plan would divert some scarce state funds from failing TPSs to private and religious schools. Failing districts are often found in poorer urban areas. The failing schools, from which the voucher students would transfer, would lose enrollment-based state and federal aid. These failing districts may be poor performing districts because they were traditionally under-resourced districts.

These districts may have become failing because they lacked the property values and tax base with which to generate the revenues necessary to provide an educational quality commensurate with affluent districts. State and federal governments may have contributed to the under-resourcing by providing aid that neither funded all students' needs nor accounted for the lack of a proper tax base.

The $10,000 tuition grant is inequitable. And this grant may be less than the per-pupil cost for religious schools and independent schools' tuition. If private, religious, or independent schools cannot reject potential voucher students even for lack of capacity, who pays the difference between the $10,000 tuition grant and religious schools' per-pupil cost or independent schools' tuition that creates inequities? Affluent parents could more easily afford to pay the difference, while requiring all parents to pay the difference would disenfranchise low-income and poor parents.

If private, religious, or independent schools are given no discretion on whether they can afford to accept voucher students, these schools might be forced to close, expand even if expansion was uneconomical, or create a two-tiered tuition scenario within the school with non-voucher students paying higher tuition to offset the voucher deficit.

Should private independent schools have discretion, they might admit only voucher students whose parents were willing to pay the tuition, fail undesirable voucher students (e.g., disciplinary records), or refuse voucher students who were more expensive to educate such as special education, ELL, and free-and-reduced-price lunch creating more inequities. Moreover, many religious schools are already financially distressed while others are closing due to budgetary pressures (see Baker, 2010).

The voucher program would create student free agents who would have an opportunity to attend a private or religious school, potentially providing a higher quality education. If the program did not require voucher students to attend their chosen school for the full academic year, these free agents could use their vouchers to transfer to another school midyear. Private or religious schools losing free agent voucher students during the year would lose voucher revenue. And these schools would experience increased costs especially if they had hired additional personnel or built more classrooms and other facilities to accommodate voucher students.

If no deadline exists by which voucher students must enroll such as by April before the upcoming school year, enrollment would be difficult to forecast, exposing operating budgets to greater risk. If private, religious, or independent schools are given no discretion on accepting vouchers students, the more desirable of these schools could suffer overcrowding and congestion. These problems could cause free agent voucher and more mobile non-voucher students to depart during the year exacerbating operating and financial problems. Housing values might plummet commensurate with increased school overcrowding. Also, enrollment increases stemming from vouchers might not be equally distributed among schools or by grade level.

If no provision is made to provide equally accessible and affordable transportation, vouchers would disproportionately benefit the affluent who can more easily afford transportation. Not all students would have equal access to private or public transportation, including public light rail. If the failing school district was required to provide or pay for voucher student transportation, failing school costs would increase especially if transportation expenses were not capped.

Failing school neighborhoods or districts depress housing values because poor school quality is negatively capitalized in housing values. Low-assessed housing values keep district property values low. Those who can vote with their feet move to districts that provide housing and schools that better meet their preferences. White or middle-class flight exacerbates the decline of neighborhoods as jobs and capital exit with them. Taxpayers are investors who want their major asset, their home, to appreciate in value. Homeowners or catchment area residents have a vested interest in the success of their local TPSs because they strive to offset the risks posed by vouchers to their community-specific social capital and property values, which cannot be easily diversified.

The voucher plan subsidizes private, religious, or independent schools at the expense of traditionally under-resourced failing TPSs. The voucher plan is not a means for improving failing schools. On the contrary, the voucher plan creates a triple assault on failing TPSs. First, the voucher plan diverts essential funds away from needy TPSs. Second, the voucher plan causes failing TPSs losing voucher students to lose state and federal enrollment-based aid. Third, failing TPSs' costs increase because costs do not decrease proportionately with lost enrollment. The more mobile and affluent voucher students may be more likely to use vouchers. Losing voucher students increases the proportions of those more expensive to educate remaining in the failing TPSs, thereby increasing costs.

If vouchers were used to their logical extreme perhaps with full funding and transportation, large high-poverty urban areas could lose students to the extent that the traditional public education system would close leaving a skeletal district. Lacking true TPSs, housing values might plummet, further eroding the tax base and increasing the exodus of the remaining relatively more mobile and affluent taxpayers. Neighborhood erosion would accelerate driving out businesses and employment. If taken to the extreme, an unfettered voucher plan could culminate in the demise of urban areas with a preponderance of failing schools.

The provision of education through local public school districts in which students who live in the district attend its TPSs enables community members to get to know and understand one another. Fischel (2002) argues this "reduces the transaction costs of citizen provision of true local public goods" such as public education (p. 1). The public benefit of children attending their local schools rather than schools in more remote areas accrues to the families living in the catchment areas. This "network of adult acquaintances," that

Fischel (2002) defines as "community-specific social capital," would be reduced to the extent voucher students left their residential district:

> The publicness of local public schools is an argument against vouchers in the following sense. By enabling parents to select schools outside their communities and outside of local public supervision, vouchers work against the neighborhood and community networks that facilitate the bottom-up provision of local public goods. Community-specific social capital is more difficult to form if members of the community send their children to schools in other communities. (p. 1)

Vouchers can also erode community-specific social capital—and, thereby, the public support necessary for proper public funding of public education.

## Charter Schools and School Choice

Governments are also allocating funds to local communities to open their own charter schools. Even Catholic communities, who have lost over half their schools and 65 percent of their enrollment (see Cooper 2015), are sometimes taking charter school funds to open and sustain their "Catholic" charter schools. Public school leaders should be aware of the growth of local charter schools, and learn from them. What do these schools offer that might be tried in local public schools?

While Catholic charter schools often lose their religious identify, the other option is often to close the school altogether—and send the kids to public schools in the neighborhood. As the Friedman Foundation (2013) states:

> The Catholic archdioceses of Indianapolis, Miami, and Washington, D.C., have closed down Catholic schools, only to reopen them as independently managed public *charter schools*. However, charter schools must strip themselves of any Catholic identity during the school day. Because of that, some have attempted to offer religious after-school programs.
>
> And many experts, such as University of Notre Dame law professor Richard Garnett, wrote at the Mirror of Justice blog, "As a general matter, I would strongly prefer that Catholic schools remain *Catholic* schools—schools where a Catholic mission and commitment pervades the entire enterprise . . . even if these charters are accompanied by various before- and after-school religious-education programs." (Carney, Friedman Foundation, 2013, p. 21)

Thus, the church–state issue is complex and active, so that local public school leaders, teachers, and parents need to be aware and expert in this field. As we discussed in a Commentary in *Education Week*, vouchers can be spent in religious schools, following the court decision in *Zelman v. Simmons-Harris* (2001):

After the U.S. Supreme Court's 2002 decision in *Zelman* v. *Simmons-Harris*, which said that public vouchers could be used for students' tuition at religious K-12 schools, the state of Minnesota allowed a Muslim group to open the Tarek ibn Ziyad Academy in Inver Grove Heights, MN.

Schools in other states could follow Ziyad Academy's example, the authors say. They offer the following tips, and others, for religious groups that may be interested: create a separate, secular foundation to support the school; adopt a mission statement that includes specific educational goals unrelated to the religious or cultural purposes; and develop a curriculum that meets the school's religious, cultural, and educational needs.

The British government has been considering making the entire school system into charters. See this view: what might happen if the United States, like the United Kingdom, were to *"charterize"* its school system, introducing family choice, private ownership, and school variety—supported by public funding? The Brits are considering the move. As Diane Ravitch (2015) recently reported from MS Campbell Brown:

> Last week, addressing his party for the first time since his re-election in May, U.K. Prime Minister David Cameron called for an end to the country's traditional public school system, endorsing instead a nationwide conversion to academies, which are essentially the British equivalent of charter schools—publicly funded, but with greater freedom over what they teach and how they are run. (p. 1)

Called "free schools," not to be confused with schools such Summerhill (see Cooper, 1971), these "academies" would replace the grammar and other schools, creating a system of government *schools that are privately run and owned but publicly funded and evaluated.* What can the United States learn and do around and from these schools?

This discussion considers some of the advantages and disadvantages of "charterizing" (creating wide chartering), privatizing, and decentralizing the U.S. education system for all. Let us consider some of the advantages first:

- **Increasing Parent Control and Choice:** Some have persuasively argued that parents need and deserve more control over their own children's education. For generations, parents have often considered the quality of local schools when selecting where to live, which neighborhoods, or which suburb. For Prime Minister Cameron urged that "current and would-be educators across the U.K.—parents, community groups, social service organizations—to create small new academies known as free schools" (Ravitch, 2015, p. 1).
- **Creating Greater Diversity of Schools:** The major private school group in the United States, the Roman Catholics, has seen their schools closing, with an enrollment that peaked in 1965 at 5.66 million students, has dropped to under 1.7 million in 2015, with no end to the decline is sight (Cooper,

2015). Perhaps if Catholic schools could become *Catholic charter schools*, this move should keep more of Catholic schools and education alive, without entangling the "church and the state." This trend has already started in the United States, with a number of Catholic schools, which were on the verge of closing, becoming charter schools to help them to save themselves.

For example, as Eliza Shapiro (2015) reported:

With Catholic schools closing across New York City and enrollment plummeting 35 percent over the last decade alone, Queen of Angels and five other Catholic schools in East Harlem and the South Bronx have banded into a "network"—another charter term—of six schools and 2,100 students to try to reverse course. (*Politico-New York*, beta, July 20, 2015)

And the concept has wide appeal in both the United States and the United Kingdom, increasing choice, funding, availability, and variety. Saving Catholic schools is an important step in the private school and religious marketplace in the United States.

The idea is that if these six schools can show substantive improvement over the next several years, the rest of the city's struggling Catholic schools could follow. And the partnership's leaders are looking to the city's high-performing charter schools as a template for their revamped schools.

- **Private Is Private, Independent Is Independent:** What are some of the advantages of being a private school in the United States? In a bureaucracy, even in education, being free has certain advantages:

  The potential benefits of private schools accrue from their independence. Private schools do not receive tax revenues, so they do not have to follow the same sorts of regulations and bureaucratic processes that govern (and sometimes hinder) public schools. This allows many private schools to be highly specialized, offering differentiated learning, advanced curriculum, or programs geared toward specific religious beliefs. There are exceptions to such generalizations— charter and magnet schools are increasingly common public schools that often have a special educational focus or theme. (GreatSchool Staff, 2015, p. 2)

Thus, public school leaders, and others, should be aware of the loosening of the restrictions and the opening of schools with a religious sponsorship that can and are supported by public funds such as vouchers. Thus, advice might include:

1. Become aware of public and private options for school support, such as vouchers and charter schools.

2. Try to compete with these schools, to keep the pupils in public schools and achieving.
3. Listen to parents' concerns and complaints that might lead to withdrawal from local public schools and movement into regional private, religious, and charter schools.

## Advice for Public School Leaders

Every school leader now needs to learn about the public–private school options, and how they are working locally, as follows:

1. *Understand the differences and similarities between public and nonpublic education in their local districts and states.*
2. *See what policies and programs are available and their history.*
3. *Look into how private school options are affecting local public schools, including enrollment and resources.*
4. *Investigate ways that public and private school can cooperate to help all students in both sectors.*

For example, in 1964, President Lyndon B. Johnson proposed the important Elementary and Secondary Education Act (ESEA), a program, to help local districts assist poor children following the integration (desegregation) policies set in the *Brown v. Board of Education* decision by the U.S. Supreme Court a decade earlier (1954, 1955). When the president needed support for his new proposed program, federal aid for low-income students, he turned to Monsignor Fredrick G. Hochwalt, a leader of the Catholic Church for political help. Catholic support mattered in Congress.

Monsignor Hochwalt offered to back ESEA if poor Catholic children and schools could and would receive similar help. So when Congress passed ESEA, Catholic schools could pay staff to help poor children, originally on public school sites with the Catholic kids taking buses to local public schools for free Title I remedial help.

As Marie Valpoon Leekley (2002) explained about Monsignor Hochwalt's work with President Lyndon Johnson,

A major issue in the century long struggle for federal aid to education was the question of federal aid to nonpublic schools. This study investigates Monsignor Frederick G. Hochwalt's effect on the Catholic position towards federal aid leading up to the enactment of the Elementary and Secondary Education Act [ESEA] of 1965. The Catholic Church had long been one of the strongest opponents of federal aid to education; however, in November of 1945 the Roman Catholic hierarchy issued a statement through the Department of Education of the National Catholic Welfare conference that signaled the beginnings of a change of attitude towards federal aid. (p. 11)

When transportation became too costly and inconvenient, it was simply easier for the public school remedial teachers to visit Catholic schools and help the kids needing and qualifying for federal assistance. Amazing to see public school teachers working in Catholic schools; and this ESEA Title I program is still operating for a half century. As *Education Week* recently explained,

> This year, we are commemorating significant milestones in our civil rights history, including the 50th anniversary of the Voting Rights Act, the 75th anniversary of the founding of the NAACP Legal Defense and Educational Fund, the 61st anniversary of the *Brown* v. *Board of Education* decision, and the 50th anniversary of the signing of the Elementary and Secondary Education Act into law.

All this happened back when civil rights, racial integration, and helping low-income students to gain a quality education, became one issue (race) and another issue (social class), and a third one (public and private) which all came together. As a school leader, one should understand and appreciate the help offered to low-income students attending (most often) Catholic schools across the nation.

Also, we should mention that the legal issue of the constitutional First Amendment, "the Separation of Church State," was tested, determining that it was both legal and democratic for low-income kids to be helped under Title I, regardless of where they went to school (public or private or religious).

At first, however, the *Aguilar v. Felton* case found that helping low-income kids in religious private schools was unconstitutional, under the "Entanglement" clause of the First Amendment that requires the "separation of Church and State." However, later, the U.S. Supreme Court reversed the decision, since helping kids in math and reading are hardly having the state pay for religious instruction:

> *Zobrest* and *Witters* make clear that, under current law, the "Shared Time" program in *Ball* and New York City's Title I program will not, as a matter of law, be deemed to have the effect of advancing religion through indoctrination. Thus, both this Court's precedent and its experience require rejection of the premises upon which *Ball* relied. (pp. 16–24)

Thus, aiding poor kids who attend private, religious schools, using public funding (Title I), is okay, as long as the in-school program is academic and not religious. In sum, for example, "New York City's Title I program does not give aid recipients any incentive to modify their religious beliefs or practices in order to obtain program services." For public school leaders, then, the following are admissible under these court decisions:

1. Federal programs can be shared among religious, private, and public schools.
2. All students deserve, need, and should receive equal help under the same and similar criteria.
3. Whether children attend a private, religious, or public school, they can get similar assistance. To remember, "The *Aguilar* Court erred in concluding that New York City's Title I program resulted in an excessive entanglement between church and state."

## Homeschooling for K-12 Kids

Finally, in this chapter, we want to understand how and why an expanding number of parents are *homeschooling* their children and to what degree is the movement growing in the United States? Two books are now available on the subject of homeschooling (Cooper, 2005; Cooper and Spielhagen, 2016), giving the numbers, reasons, and forces behind this homeschool movement.

After all, almost all children to some degree are "homeschooled," as their parents (and grandparents) rear, support, and love them, and hope that their kids will be and do well. From these early beginnings, the number of U.S. children who are homeschooled has increased over the years, as discussed by Brian Ray, in this current report:

> There are about 2.2 million home-educated students in the United States. They were an estimated 1.73 to 2.35 million children (in grades K to 12) home educated during the spring of 2010 in the United States It appears the homeschool population is continuing to grow (at an estimated 2% to 8% per annum over the past few years). (Ray, 2016, p. 22)

Thus, school leaders should be aware of the homeschooling option: keeping up with kids who withdraw from their local schools—and are educated at home. Just because certain children are being homeschooled does not mean that these kids are excluded from public school activities and programs. For example, a number of states and localities now allow and encourage homeschoolers to join their local school teams and after-school activities.

## The Tebow Case

Take the interesting case of Tim Tebow, a well-known football star. Recently, a bill in Virginia—the so-called Tebow Bill—was *vetoed* by Governor Terry

McAuliffe (Democrat), a law that "would have allowed local homeschoolers to participate in athletics" at their local *public* schools. As the sponsor of the defeated bill, David Ramadan (R-Loudon) explained, "Affording our constituents' kids the opportunity to play sports at their schools, schools that their parents pay taxes to build [and operate] is simply a fairness issue" (Batman, 2015, p. 9).

Thus, while Virginia has said "no" to homeschoolers' participating in local public school sports (and some other extracurricular activities), the Home School Legal Defense Association reported that nine other states do have sports participation enablement laws, including, Arizona, Colorado, Florida, Idaho, Iowa, Maine, North Dakota, Oregon, and Washington.

Often these state homeschool eligibility laws are interestingly called "Tebow Laws," named for Tim Tebow, a National Football League player for the Florida Gators and New York Jets—and a Heisman Trophy winner—who was homeschooled in Florida and played football for his local public high school team. Tebow, born in the Philippines, was homeschooled by his parents who were Baptist missionaries.

Laws are important—and their interpretation is too—even in determining whether kids can play a team sport for a public school in their home communities. Take a look at the local districts programs and policies that affect (and include or not) local homeschoolers. See how they affect the local schools and kids. Just because a family decides to homeschool their offspring does not mean that parents do not want their kids to participate, make friends, learn activities, and have the important experience of teamwork. And parents still must pay their local taxes, much of which goes for local education.

Explore and perhaps do the following as a school leader:

1. *Check local educational policies and programs for all children, including those who are being homeschooled.*
2. *See whether kids in local schools are participating and in what sports and activities.*
3. *Decide and take action, to include all interested children, even someone like Tim Tebow, who was homeschooled, played for the local public high school, and went on to be an outstanding professional athlete and has an award named after him.*
4. *Consult lawyers if any issue arises that might be affecting students in the community or school and their access to local sports and other school activities (band, orchestra, service clubs).*
5. *Remember, all children have needs to be involved, affiliated and active in sports activities and programs, even if their parents selected a homeschooling option; these parents are still paying taxes, including local property taxes, and thus are supporting local public education—even if their kids are kept home for their education.*

# REFERENCES

Aalbers, M. B. (2011). *Place, exclusion, and mortgage markets*. Malden, MA: Wiley-Blackwell.

Baker, B. D. (March 23, 2010). *Would $8,000 scholarships help sustain NJ private schools?* [Web log post]. Available at http://schoolfinance101.wordpress.com/2010/3/23/ would_$8,000_scholarships_help_sustain_NJ_private_schools?

(Batman, 2015, p. 9). "https://web.archive.org/web/20151217145608/http://vcdl.org/sites/default/files/General_Assembly_Voting_Score_for_2015.pdf"Virginia Citizens Defense League: 2015 Scorecard: Legislators are scored on their votes on bills related to the second amendment. (David Ramadan, 2015).

(Batman, 2015, p. 9). "http://dela.state.va.us/dela/MemBios.nsf/a7b082ef6ed01e-ac85256c0d00515644/b992dd6f4701ceec85257535005773fd?OpenDocument&Click=85256823005F1997.f0a3d2c6f9f07af1852570bd00646e36/$Body/0.1A96" "Virginia House of Delegates 2013; Delegate David I. Ramadan". Virginia House of Delegates. Retrieved 2013-04-16.

Carr, J. H., & Kutty, N. K. (2008). *Segregation*. New York: Routledge, Taylor & Francis Group.

*Catholic Education Daily*. (2014). Catholic Schools 'Switching' to Charter Schools, Study Finds, May 19, 2014, at 11:46 AM 5/19/2014. | By CNS Staff |

Cattaro, G. M., & Russo, C. J. (Eds.) (2015). *Gravissimum educationis: Golden opportunities in American Catholic education 50 years after Vatican II*. Lanham, MD: Rowman & Littlefield.

Coons, J. E., Sugarman, S. D., & Clune, W. H. (1970). *Private wealth and public education*. Cambridge, MA: Belknap Press of Harvard University Press.

Cooper, B. S. (1971). *Free and freedom schools: A national survey of alternative programs*. Washington, DC: President' Commission on School Finance.

Cooper, B. S. (2005). *Home schooling in full view: A reader*. Charlotte, NC: Information Age Publishing.

Cooper, B. S. (2015). Faith-based education: Ecumenical schools and their implications for the future of American Catholic education in *Gravissimum Educationis: Golden opportunities in American Catholic education 50 years after Vatican II*. G. M. Cattaro & C. J., Eds. Lanham, MD: Rowman & Littlefield.

Cooper, B. S., & Spielhagen, F. (2016), *Homeschooling in new view*. Charlotte, NC: Information Age Publishing.

Cooper, B. S., & Zhu, M. (2016). Faith-based schools: Ecumenical schools and their implications for the future of American Catholic education, Chapter 8 in *Gravissimum educationis: Golden opportunities in American Catholic education 50 years after Vatican II*. Gerald Cattaro & Charles Russo, Eds. Lanham, MD: Rowman & Littlefield.

Fischel, W. A. (1998). *School finance litigation and property tax revolts: How undermining local control turns voters away from public education*. Lincoln Institute of Land Policy Working Paper, Cambridge, MA, USA.

Fischel, W. A. (2001). *The home voter hypothesis: How home values influence local government taxation, school finance, and land-use policies*. Cambridge, MA: Harvard University Press.

Fischel, W. A. (2002). *An economic case against vouchers: Why local public schools are a local public good.* Dartmouth Economics Department Working Paper, Dartmouth College, Hanover, NH, USA.

Fischel, W. A. (2005). *Why voters veto vouchers: Public schools and community-specific social capital.* Dartmouth Economics Department Working Paper, Dartmouth College, Hanover, NH, USA.

Freund, D. M. P. (2010). *Colored property.* Chicago, IL: University of Chicago Press.

Friedman Foundation (2013). *Catholic schools benefit from converting to charter schools study finds* by Gina Cairney.

Hoxby, C. M. (2001). All school finance equalizations are not created equal. *Quarterly Journal of Economics, 116*(4), pp. 1189–231.

Jackson, K. T. (1985). *Crabgrass frontier: The suburbanization of the United States.* New York, NY: Oxford University Press.

Ladd, H. F. (1976). Statewide taxation of commercial and industrial property for education. *National Tax Journal, 29*(2), pp. 143–53.

Ladson-Billings, G. (2006). From the achievement gap to the education debt: Understanding achievement in U.S. schools. *Educational Researcher, 35*(7), pp. 3–12.

Leekley, Marie Valpoon. (January 1, 2002). *A study of Monsignor Frederick G. Hochwalt and the Catholic Church's position towards federal aid. Dissertations, 1996–2001.* Paper AAI3061524. Available at http://epublications.marquette.edu/dissertations/ AAI3061524.

Metzler, J. (2003). Inequitable equilibrium: School finance in the United States. *Indiana Law Review, 36*(3), 561–608.

National Council of State Legislatures. (NCSL, 2015). *School voucher laws: State by state comparison.* Washington, DC: NCSL.

Prothero, A. (2014). Converting Catholic schools to charters draws scrutiny. *Education Week, 30*(1), pp. 55–56.

Ray, Brian. (2016). Chapter one, pp. 4–14 in *Homeschooling in New View.* Cooper, B. S., & Spielhagen, F. Charlotte, NC: Information Age Publishing.

Ravitch, Diane. (October 17, 2015). "Campbell Brown Calls for Elimination of All Public Schools." Diane Ravitch Blog, pp. 1–3.

Shapiro, Eliza. (2015). "Facing decline, Catholic schools form a charter-like network." *Politico-New York.*

Sharp, G. (November 30, 2008). *1934 Philadelphia redlining map.* Available at http://www.thesocietypages.org.

Squires, G. D. (2003). Racial profiling, insurance style: Insurance redlining and the uneven development of metropolitan areas. *Journal of Urban Affairs, 25*(4), pp. 391–410.

Squires, G. D., & Kubrin, C. E. (2005). Privileged places: Race, uneven development, and the geography of opportunity in urban America. *Urban Studies, 42*(1), pp. 47–68.

*Chapter 11*

# School Finance for Principals

## *Money May Be Green but Financial Policy Should Be Transparent*

### David Alan Dolph

## INTRODUCTION

Principals must complete a variety of duties if they are to be successful in providing quality education for their students, striking a balance between focusing on leadership and management, including finance. Certainly, principals must emphasize instructional leadership by developing visions aimed at improving the school, teaching and learning, increasing student test scores, growing learning communities, and encouraging collaborative school cultures. At the same time, though, principals must be adept at basic managerial functions. A critical aspect of school management, then, focuses on principals' ability to manage fiscal resources.

In light of increasingly limited resources and higher expectations about providing quality programs, it is essential for school administrators, including principals, to have working knowledge and skill about management of available resources. Stakeholders expect and demand expertise and trustworthiness from public servants, including educators.

Insofar as education is big business in most communities, schooling utilizes large amounts of public tax dollars. It is therefore imperative for educators to maintain high levels of accountability as to how to spend public resources. Moreover, in today's climate of reduced resources, there is public demand for school improvement, with high expectations that money spent on education will yield positive results, not only for students but also for communities at large. In order to demonstrate improvement, schools need sufficient resources necessary to provide programs geared toward higher levels of student achievement, including test scores. However, school improvement often involves changes in school operations, programs, and processes. New initiatives making differences often require additional fiscal resources in order to be implemented. If schools are to achieve their missions, goals, and objectives, principals must exhibit wise fiscal stewardship of limited available dollars in order to succeed.

Financing public education is a combined enterprise involving local, state, and federal resources. The burden of overall fiscal management for school systems typically falls on central office personnel such as superintendents, treasurers, and business managers along with tasks such as managing tax referenda, budgeting, accounting, and monitoring district expenditures, salaries, benefits, employee negotiations, district operating, and capital budgets. Even so, it is important for principals to have sufficient knowledge about budgeting, accounting, legal issues, and other fiscally related matters pertaining to schools in order to serve as credible school officials in the eyes of the public.

By role and function, insofar as principals serve as primary intermediaries between schools and communities, they should be able to provide accurate explanations of school-related fiscal issues to interested stakeholders. Principals should be able to engage in realistic and informed discussions with central office personnel in order to explain and lobby for resources to support educational programs in their buildings. Due to the need to understand overriding financial issues such as where fiscal resources come from and basic school site issues related to school finance, this chapter provides information principals should be competent and aware of in order to be successful practitioners.

Because laws and school policies dictate multiple functions carried on by school systems, principals must understand the macro aspects influencing finance as well as micro issues affecting their functions in both leading and managing their buildings.

By providing general information about state funding at the district and individual building levels related to school funding, the chapter is designed to provide principals with insight into improved knowledge, skill, and dispositions.

Against this background, the remainder of this chapter is divided into six sections. The chapter initially discusses factors affecting varying levels of principals' involvement in fiscal decisions in schools. Second, the chapter briefly reviews examples of litigation affecting school funding because even though this information is typically beyond the purview of principals, it is useful for them to have basic knowledge of how their states' funding models came to be so they can explain them to teachers, staff, and other stakeholders.

Consequently, the chapter explores five influential school funding cases in relation to how states modified funding approaches for schools resulting from legal challenges. And, the chapter reviews the sources of where funding for school systems come from. Fourth, the chapter delves into areas principals are responsible for, including financial issues, typically encountered on daily basis. Fifth, the chapter offers ten recommendations for principals to consider. Finally, the chapter offers concluding thoughts.

By providing general information about state funding for schools, and how resources are then used at the district and building levels, the chapter hopes to provide principals with insight into improved knowledge, skill, and dispositions.

## Factors Affecting Principals' Involvement in Finance

The extent of involvement in fiscal management by principals varies considerably from one school system to another. Kowalski (2010) attributes this variability to three factors. The first differentiator is the philosophical approach toward organizational structure prevalent in districts. Whether the predominant approach towards organizational structure in a district is centralized or decentralized affects the levels of principal involvement in financial decisions.

Not surprisingly, centralized models focus control at central office levels in districts where the locus of power and decision-making resides with educational leaders such as superintendents, treasurers, and business managers. In addition, this model effectively reduces principal autonomy and control in decision-making regarding fiscal and educational issues.

Centralized organizational structures favor central office control over school-based functions including fiscally related decisions on resource allocation. The advantages of centralized organizational systems include uniformity for district operations and lessening of managerial responsibilities for principals, thus freeing them to focus on instructional leadership.

The disadvantages of centralization include the use of one-size-fits-all approaches that do not necessarily apply to every building in districts. Further, the reduced involvement by building principals that emerges under a centralized model may result in a lack of support for financial decisions and clearly diminish the power and control granted at building levels.

A second model for school system organizational structure is decentralization or site-based management (SBM). SBM in schools blossomed, in part, due to court-ordered changes mandated, particularly in Kentucky (Russo, 1994–1995). SBM was linked to school movements emerging in the 1990s, although early forerunners of SBM budgeting were initiated in Detroit and New York during the 1970s in an attempt to decentralize the budgets within the larger school districts (White, 1989; Wissler and Ortiz, 1986). While these earlier attempts in Detroit and New York focused on decentralizing school-based budgeting, they did not include school-based decision-making (White, 1989; Wissler and Ortiz, 1986).

Site-based approaches favoring decentralized organizational structures are in line with the principle of subsidiarity, according to which the best decisions are made closest to the levels at which they are to be implemented. SBM, as opposed to centralized models of organizational structure, favor decision-making at school building levels in the majority of programmatic decisions, including those related to fiscal management. SBM is a strategy often cited as a model for school improvement (Giles et al., 2005).

School-based budgeting recognizes the importance of the impact of resources at the point of use (Thompson and Wood, 2005). Moreover, SBM budgeting is popular because it involves stakeholders at individual school sites. Involvement of building-level stakeholders, including teachers, staff, and parents is beneficial because one of the hallmarks of successful schools is parental involvement (Giles et al., 2005; Stringer and Hourani, 2013).

Under school-based budgeting models, individual school buildings receive financial resources based on formulas or policies usually based on the numbers of students they serve (Thompson and Wood, 2005). Buildings with greater numbers of pupils receive more financial resources to support educational programming than schools with fewer students. SBM fiscal management asserts the view that financial resources are best spent in classrooms supporting teaching and learning.

As popular as SBM may be, the model has limitations and disadvantages. One of the chief difficulties posed by SBM is its need for higher levels of expertise on the part of principals regarding budgeting, accounting, and auditing. For principals, engaging in finance-related management activities requires time away from instructional leadership and may have a deleterious effect on teaching and learning. Further, including more people into decision-making processes may complicate matters due to varying opinions on where financial resources should be allocated.

Equity is another issue that may suffer in site-based approaches because some principals are more aggressive and skilled in acquiring resources. This results in increased disparity in available resources, leading to unequal educational opportunities for students. Nevertheless, models of organizational structures are a major factor in determining the extent of principal involvement in school finance issues.

The second feature influencing the levels of principal involvement in fiscal matters is school size. Often, principals in smaller schools may be less involved in fiscal management than their counterparts in larger schools (Kowalski, 2010). Additionally, smaller schools usually have reduced budgets due to lesser needs based on fewer students and staff. Also, smaller school districts usually do not have administrators designated as business managers. Superintendents and treasurers at central office levels control most fiscal matters for small schools and systems. Moreover, in larger districts, it is possible for principals to have assistant principals assigned to areas involving fiscal responsibility. Consequently, school size issues may impact how involved principals are in overall financial planning and management.

The third factor affecting the levels of principal involvement in fiscal matters is related to board policy and individual job descriptions. Both policy and job descriptions can determine what administrators are allowed and required to do in relation to acquiring and allocating resources. Because policies vary from one school system to another, principals should understand basic tenets of fiscal management in order to be successful in any type of school building, regardless of structure, size, or job descriptions. This is not to suggest that all principals must become experts in school finance. Rather, principals should have a fundamental grasp of resource acquisition, budgeting, accounting, and auditing in order to manage their schools successfully from a resource perspective.

## School Funding Litigation

Principals customarily are not engaged in fiscal activities at district levels. Because they have not traditionally been participants in discussions at central offices about resource allocation, principals may not be aware of how their state finance systems function or were developed. Even so, because principals may be called on to discuss or respond to questions from staff, parents, and/or community members related to these topics, it is essential for them to have fundamental understandings of their states funding model.

Funding models or formulas are compilations of laws enacted by state legislative systems to distribute resources to school systems. Although principals are not usually involved in how these models work, they are impacted by the result of resource distribution to their schools.

Regardless of the process in place in individual states, the backbone of most revenue for schools in the United States has been on real property taxes since the 1800s (Owings and Kaplan, 2006). One inherent difficulty with this source of revenue is that school systems have varying values of real property to tax at their disposal. In other words, districts located in areas of low property value are unlikely to be able to generate as much revenue as those in property-rich areas. This inequity leads to the potential for uneven levels of funding available for schools used in support of educational programs.

Two critical concepts relative to school funding are equity and adequacy. Odden and Picus (2014) describe equity as referring to providing students with basically equal educational resources plus additional resources required for special situations such as students with disabilities or with limited English capabilities. Adequacy refers to whether school systems receive enough funding to provide their students with educations attaining appropriate levels of quality. Both of these concepts are major factors in school funding litigation.

Insofar as the central issue in school finance involves supporting schools with sufficient levels of fiscal resources to fund educational programs, perceptions related to lack of equity and adequacy in schools has led to judicial challenges because aggrieved parties believe they are not getting their fair share of resources. Consequently, many school funding models have been altered due to litigation.

The constitutionality of state funding systems is the principle area challenged by individuals or groups who are aggrieved regarding school funding. Insofar as the Tenth Amendment of the U.S. Constitution is silent as to education, it is a reserved power of the states. As a result, states determine the means of financing education through their own constitutions and related statutes. Moreover, the federal government continues to play a larger role in public education as reflected in such statutes such as the Individuals with Disabilities Education Act (2005) and the Every Student Succeeds Act (ESSA) (2015).

Thro (2013) identified three waves of school litigation. During the first wave, reflected in *Serrano v. Priest I* (1971) (*Serrano I*) and *San Antonio v. Rodriguez* (1973), plaintiffs alleged primarily that all children were not being treated equally in violation of the Equal Protection Clause of the Fourteenth Amendment to the U.S. Constitution. In *Serrano I*, the Supreme Court of California, reversing an earlier order to the contrary, ruled that insofar as the state's system of school funding discriminated against poor students because the quality of the education they received depended on the wealth of the districts in which they lived, it violated their rights to equal protection.

Two years later, in its only case on school finance, *San Antonio v. Rodriguez* (1973) a dispute from Texas, the Supreme Court essentially repudiated *Serrano I*. The Court held that Texas's funding model did not violate the Equal Protection Clause because the U.S. Constitution does not mention education. According to the Justices, "[e]ducation, of course, is not among the rights afforded explicit protection under our Federal Constitution. Nor do we find any basis for saying it is implicitly so protected" (*San Antonio*, 1973, p, 35). The effect of *San Antonio* was that future school finance cases would have to be argued based on individual state equal protection or education clauses.

The second wave of school funding litigation argued in state courts targeted inequalities in funding based on violations of individual state constitutions, focusing largely on equity theories (Thro, 2013). *Robinson v. Cahill* (1973), which originated in New Jersey, was a key second wave case based on the notion of fundamentality of education as a right because students in poorer districts were being deprived of quality educational opportunities.

In its judgment, the court ignored the influence of *San Antonio*, instead calling into play the state constitutional provision requiring a thorough and efficient educational system in public schools due to unequal resource inputs per pupil. Further, in *Serrano v. Priest* (1976) (*Serrano II*), the Supreme Court of California was of the opinion that absent of a compelling justification, the state could not discriminate in the quality of school services made available to the students. *Serrano II* affirmed reliance on language in its state constitution as bases for litigation, thus insulating *Serrano II* from *San Antonio*.

The third wave of cases focused on issues related to educational adequacy. As noted, adequacy differs from equity insofar as equity refers to each child receiving equal educational resources while adequacy requires that all schools receive sufficient funding required to provide educational opportunities for students that meet defined levels of quality (Odden and Picus, 2014).

One of the most influential cases using adequacy was *Rose v. Council of Better Education* (1989). *Rose* is a landmark because it emphasizes the importance of states' responsibilities to provide sufficient educational opportunities to allow them to attain defined standards of educational quality. In *Rose*, the court decided that Kentucky's entire education system was unconstitutional. The commonwealth was then required to complete an overhaul of its education system along with restructuring the funding system in order to provide an adequate education for all students.

The net result of the three waves of school funding reform is that they eventually led to where we are today, namely, along with providing resources for schools, there is an expectation of positive outcomes for students. Consequently, much of the accountability schools now face stems from the evolution of school finance litigation linking fiscal resources or inputs to educational outcomes or outputs.

School finance litigation has filled volumes of books and articles. While, of course, principals are not required to be experts in all of these cases or areas, it would be helpful if they have working knowledge and awareness of the history of these cases, particularly ones that are relevant in their states. This can be helpful information for principals to possess when stakeholders ask questions related to funding. Additionally, principals should have general understanding of various sources of income for school districts, a topic the chapter next examines.

## Where Does the Money Come From?

Three primary revenue streams are available to school boards. The revenue sources coming from, state, local, and federal levels, all rely on some form of taxation. In addition, boards may receive additional revenue from areas such as investments, donations, and grants; still, the bulk of school revenue stems from the three areas just identified.

To reiterate, the primary source of district revenue stems from real property taxation within localities where school districts are located. The only exception to this is in Michigan, which uses sales tax (Mich. Comp. Laws Ann. §388.1620). There is no uniform approach to this process; instead, over time, states have developed financial formulas, sometimes known as foundation plans (Carey, 2002).

As an example, Ohio utilizes a foundation formula that typically makes up the majority of revenue for schools. The money in the foundation formula comes from the state's General Revenue Fund as well as a lottery fund (http://www.lsc.ohio.gov/schoolfunding/edufeb2015.pdf).

The second primary source of income is local sources acquired by taxation acquired typically through referenda. From a local perspective, school systems can generate additional funds through referenda based on property taxes, and in some states, such as Ohio, through income taxes Ohio Revised Code (ORC 5748.1).

The third primary source for school district revenue is the federal government. The federal government provides about 8 percent of funding nationally for elementary and secondary educational institutions (U.S. Department of Education, 2016). A recent example of federal support for education is demonstrated through support for such laws as the ESSA (2015).

The federal government provides revenue through three general areas to school systems. The first of these is a categorical aid, money allocated for specific purposes. Examples of federal categorical aid include money given for special education programs, technology, and gifted and talented programs (Smith et al., 2013).

The second component of federal funding is block grants, lump sums of money given to school systems or other governmental entities for use in general purposes (FederalGrants.com, 2016). A distinguishing characteristic of block grants is that they provide schools with more flexibility and discretion as to how funds can be used.

The third source of money from the federal government is general federal aid, money to be used totally at the discretion of local school districts, assuming the use is within prescribed guidelines (Herman and Herman, 1997).

An additional category for some possible income for schools is money generated through activities such as business partnerships, foundations, and rentals of facilities to community groups. Although most boards and/or buildings attempt to increase funding through these and other auxiliary ideas, the dollars generated are generally not consistently available due to the nature of the sources. Even so, revenue from some of the underlying activities can help them to be financially self-sufficient.

Finally, although not directly related to income, in-kind services or gifts are possible bases for resources. For instance, individual buildings and districts occasionally benefit from one-time donations of items such as computers or other equipment that have allowed them to repurpose dollars in other ways. Even though these resources are not necessarily primary sources, they can be helpful in some circumstances as long as school officials understand that these situations are not sustainable.

Regardless of the source of income, it is helpful for principals to have a grasp of where revenue comes from in order to fund programs in their school districts and buildings. Armed with this information, principals can be better prepared about how to carry out their responsibilities while exercising wise fiscal stewardship in their buildings.

## Principals' Responsibilities

Principals have a multitude of responsibilities to complete in order to lead their buildings successfully in providing students with quality educational opportunities. Today's principals are faced with an ever-increasing array of professional role expectations that they are to master in their job performance as building administrators.

Over the past forty years, major school reform models have attempted to transform public education to better meet the demands and expectations of the American public, business leaders, legislators, and politicians. As a result of the various school reform efforts, the expectations placed on principals have evolved. Examples of tasks today's principals are required to perform include making daily decisions, as well as long-term decisions; overseeing the operations and personnel of the school; facilitating reform initiatives; communicating with students, parents, and faculty members regularly; disciplining students; designing creative new programs while restructuring old ones; staying professionally current; and managing school budgets.

Academicians emphasizing the importance of leadership activities such as visioning, culture building, and instruction may sometimes denigrate issues related to management, including fiscal management, yet none of the proceeding areas can occur without adequate resources. Managing resources wisely is critical in order for school officials to carry out their missions and accomplish their goals and objectives. In fact, Standard 3 from the Educational Leadership Constituencies Council (ELCC), one of six standards developed to assist current and future school administrators meet the changing demands of society and school, lists the following as important for building level administrators:

> **ELCC Standard 3.0:** A building-level education leader applies knowledge that promotes the success of every student by ensuring the management of the school organization, operation, and resources through monitoring and evaluating

school management and operational systems; efficiently using human, fiscal, and technological resources in a school environment; promoting and protecting the welfare and safety of school students and staff; developing school capacity for distributed leadership; and ensuring that teacher and organizational time focuses on high-quality instruction and student learning. (National Policy Board for Educational Administration, 2011, p. 13)

Principals need to be skilled in budgeting and finance in order to insure quality educational opportunities are provided to students. Because school finances influence every facet of district operations, the chapter shifts its focus on the specific role of principals regarding school finances. Insofar as school principals have a multitude of roles and demands on their time, finance can sometimes be viewed as less significant when it comes to their most immediate job responsibilities of improving teaching and learning. Nevertheless, it is important for principals to be aware of and to understand fully their roles in the budgeting and financial processes, as this is a critical component of effective management.

To insure successful fiscal management, particularly at building levels, principals must be knowledgeable and skilled in areas of budgeting, accounting, and auditing. In addition, there are specific areas principals need to be aware of such as managing fund-raising activities, booster accounts, and other school functions specific to building levels. Principals must have general understandings of basic elements associated in these areas in order to be successful managers of buildings.

As discussed earlier, the primary responsibility for fiscal management resides at central office levels because the majority of resources stem from state, local, and federal sources. These resources all flow to district levels, not individual buildings. Still, principals have major roles in school finance as it relates to successful building management. Because resources are distributed to the buildings that principals manage, it is imperative for principals to understand basic fundamentals related to school finance beyond simply understanding their states funding model. As a result, the chapter now considers the three broad aspects of fiscal management of which principals should be aware.

## Budgeting

Depending on the district, principals may have direct roles in developing board and building budgets. Regardless of their level of involvement, principals and their schools are directly affected by budgeting decisions. It is imperative for principals to understand, manage, and be able to explain school budgets and fiscal decisions based on available resources to stakeholders, including teachers, staff, and parents. This is particularly important during times of change, especially if innovations are driven by new legislative models of forcing resource allocation. Changes in organizational practice are usually better received if those affected understand reasons for changes.

Budgeting is an essential organizational function. In school systems, budgeting results in planning documents describing how and where fiscal resources are to be deployed to support educational plans. Budgeting is the process of gathering and understanding all sources of board revenues and all of their expenses, then, using this information to plan future expenditures related to school instruction, facilities, and school operations. Because school finances are linked with every facet of district operations, it is one of the most important considerations in the leadership and management function within their schools for principals.

Drake and Roe (1994) suggest that school budgets translate educational needs into financial plans shared with school stakeholders and community members. Further, budgets describe the parameters of educational programs to be supported by communities. In this way, budgets are legal documents justifying expenditure of public dollars.

Budgets have four functions (Odden and Picus, 2014). First, they communicate school board philosophies, while serving as policy documents. Second, budgets provide financial plans revealing both history and future intent. Third, they act as guides to operation. Fourth, budgets serve as a means of communication how public dollars are spent.

Thompson and Wood (2005) emphasize how budgets define the importance of school programs because they explain in detail educational priorities in terms of programs and resources. Budgets can also serve as political tools by describing where resources are allocated and what communities and boards of education are willing to support.

School budgets are combinations of three types of distinct planning: educational, revenue acquisition, and expenditures (Ray, Candoli, and Hack, 2005). Although the amount of principal involvement in budgeting processes varies, one area that principals are typically highly involved in relates to educational plans. Educational plans provide goals and objectives for teaching and learning. Additionally, educational plans provide reasons for establishing programs aimed at addressing missions and goals of school systems. Therefore, principals serving as building instructional leaders should have considerable involvement and influence in the development of these plans.

Ray, Candoli, and Hack (2005) note that in some cases budgets are mechanical documents developed to comply with state laws having little relation to educational plans or are devised at the administrative level with little or no input from building personnel or community stakeholders. Both approaches are shortsighted because principals need to be sensitive to the idea that budgets have both educational and economic dimensions, as well as political overtones (Kowalski, 2010).

It is worth repeating that budgets represent plans of how money is to be spent. Further, it all but goes without saying that organizations spend their financial resources on what they value as essential to fulfilling their visions, missions, and goals. Consequently, in districts and in individual buildings, budgets are plans designed to declare and define what is valued along with how precious resources are allocated. In this way, budgets serve as vehicles for communicating priorities including educational programs and plans.

Drake and Roe (1994) suggest that budgeting develops plans of activity for short and long-term organizational activities. Budgeting also necessitates evaluations of past activities as well as developing future goals, objectives, and priorities. The level of involvement of building principals is an organizational determination made by central office administrators. Principals will be more engaged in budgeting and other fiscal management in districts organized around decentralization, meaning that many decisions are made at school buildings by principals and teachers rather than central office personnel.

Thompson and Wood (2005) point out that in school-based budgeting models of budgeting, individual buildings are allocated resources based on a predetermined formulas of some sort. Generally, formulas used in this process take into account numbers of students, staff, and programs as criteria to determine how much money schools will receive. After dollars are received, it is up to the principals and their teams at individual school sites to determine how those resources are spent. The range of discretion and areas for allocation of resources may go from limited to extreme. Examples of areas warranting expenditures include supplies, equipment, programs, professional development, infrastructure modifications, and salaries.

Financial decisions regarding finances certainly must fall within guidelines established through board policy; employee-negotiated agreements; and federal, state, or local guidelines. Even so, SBM budgeting processes respect and validate the concept that the best way to determine the allocation of resources is to make it nearest the location of activity, namely individual school buildings.

Of course, the goals behind school-based budgeting and site-based budgeting are to improve educational opportunities and outcomes for all students. However, evidence of improved outcomes resulting from SBM budgeting methods has been spotty (Odden, Wohlstetter, and Odden, 1995). Still, SBM budgeting has advantages including maximum levels of stakeholder involvement, thus gaining support of budget plans, and input offered by those closest to the scene of instruction, classrooms.

School-based budgeting allows those with the highest levels of understanding of local contexts to have decision-making authority. This approach fosters better control of school-level data while offering higher levels of individual building accountability (Rennie Center for Education Research & Policy, 2012).

Disadvantages of SBM include the amount of time required, not only in the process itself but also in the necessary training of participants in order to understand and be successful. In addition, as more school site leaders have authority over financial and other types of decision-making, conflicts may arise. Hadderman (1999) cautions that implementing SBM can be difficult because it requires increased participation by stakeholders as well as principals in order to gather firsthand knowledge of programmatic needs. This, in itself, can be daunting due to time limitations, complicated paper trail processes, limited skills of most participants in the process when it comes to school finance, lack of enthusiasm, and potential conflicts arising from differing opinions on how to allocate funding. Consequently, district officials must consider the pros and cons of implementing SBM before deciding on which budgeting model to employ in districts.

## Accounting

Accounting is a second function related to good fiscal management. Kowalski (2010) identifies the purpose of accounting procedures in school systems as being designed to minimize carelessness, inappropriate expenditures, and inappropriate or illegal actions on the part of personnel. At the same time, accounting should increase improved efficiency and effectiveness as to where resources are expended. Ray, Candoli, and Hack (2005) believe that good accounting procedures help in relating monetary expenditures to educational programmatic goals. Accounting also meets state legal requirements for accountability, while providing data to school stakeholders regarding the use of taxpayer dollars.

Administrative decision-making should be improved when educational leaders utilize valid accounting practices. Leaders make better decisions when they consider where dollars have previously been spent, and how many remain for future use. Drake and Roe (1994) specify that school-based accounting systems should provide good record keeping, verification that cash receipts are handled correctly, that good practice is used with check writing and other fiscal activity, and that there is a system of checks and balances related to spending money. Because budgets are expressions of educational planning for school systems, and accounting verifies allocation of dollars, valid accounting procedures help insure that financial resources are utilized according to educational plans and programs.

It is extremely important for all school personnel charged with handling money to have clear understandings of all procedures addressing receiving and expending those resources. Informed, knowledgeable, and accountable personnel are essential if schools are to successfully demonstrate fiduciary responsibility with public money. Principals are responsible to make sure that staff members entrusted with these functions are trained. Thus, accounting processes, correctly performed, help principals manage this area of school operations making sure that procedures for doing so are accomplished legally and accurately.

## Auditing

Kowalski (2010) describes auditing as an extension or follow-up to accounting processes. Auditing procedures are used to verify levels of accuracy and completeness of financial activity in organizations. School personnel may perform audits in most instances; state auditors remain involved to make sure boards are accurately discharging their responsibilities regarding taxpayer dollars and other resources. For example, in Ohio, state auditors perform annual reviews of all financial activity in districts to ensure that school officials are complying with related state law (Ohio Revised Code, §117.11).

Auditing procedures examine school activity in terms of efficiency and cost-effectiveness. Brimley and Garfield (2008) explain that the goal of audits is to ensure that appropriate district personnel approve expenditures that receipts are accurately recorded, that purchasing processes such as purchase orders and other financial transactions are performed properly, and that bank statements are accurate. Auditing processes should present some assurances that the financial transactions and paperwork reviewed are in order, presented fairly in respect to financial reporting frameworks, and offer reasonably clear pictures of the financial status of those areas audited.

Educational leaders in school systems, including principals, must demonstrate fidelity to wise fiscal stewardship over taxpayer dollars. If principals hope to acquire additional fiscal resources in the future, they must demonstrate good fiscal management. Because principals often serve as the best connector between communities and schools, it is essential that they understand finance as it relates to school operations. It is also imperative for principals to handle the myriad of individual building-level responsibilities related to finance in order to provide optimal utilization of resources for teachers to teach and students to learn. For this reason, the chapter now examines issues directly related to principals in relation to fiscal management at building levels.

## Other Areas for Principals' Financial Involvement

Principals are normally involved in financial activities such as purchasing equipment, supplies, and other materials used in their buildings. The processes used in relation to purchasing are developed, communicated, and implemented through board policy and administrative guidelines. Typically, principals have the authority to determine the appropriateness of requests and send them to central office administrators who indicate whether sufficient funding is available.

At the same time, schools may have independent accounts that principals need to manage, the most prevalent of which address extracurricular activities. Examples of other activities may include intramurals, athletics, band, choir, intramurals, clubs, and drama. Funds may also deal with rental of facilities, school breakfast and lunch programs, school stores, vending machines, petty cash, and fundraising. Further, principals must monitor donations, student fundraisers, parent–teacher organization funds, student picture sales, yearbook sales, and many other financial transactions unique to each school building.

All of these areas require principals to adhere to written procedures developed by school boards, sound business practices, and ongoing reviews of activities (Mutter and Parker, 2004). Mutter and Parker (2004) suggest that principals must carefully manage how monies are collected, deposits are made, and receipts given. Principals must also be aware of the processes required to issue checks and purchase orders. Kowalski (2010) emphasizes that principals need to ensure that money taken in is recorded properly, use sound accounting procedures, deposit funds appropriately, make appropriate expenditures, and rely on periodic auditing.

Serving in their roles as managers, principals are expected to oversee, lead, and coordinate all school-related funds. Some school building accounts flow from district central offices and specify the budget line item with dollar amounts to be spent on a range of supplies and activities. Additional district funds may be allocated to individual schools for school-based decisions regarding how funds will be spent. These funds are typically budgeted for academic supplies, paper, educational equipment, and special programs.

It is important for principals to be aware of how funds are collected, spent, and accounted for. According to Kessler, Snodgrass, and Davis (2015), "The color of money may be green, but the color of your monetary policies must be crystal clear" (p. 40). Moreover, these authors remind principals that one of the quickest ways for principals and other educational leaders to get in serious trouble and have their names on the local news headlines is to make mistakes with money. School funds belong to the public and the principal's role is to make sure that there are clear policies in place to insure these funds are spent according to the purpose they were intended.

Each of these financial accounts may also cause significant amounts of legal and political concerns for schools and principals if they are not handled correctly. It is important for school boards and principals to have safeguards in place in the form of checks and balances to ensure these accounts are handled correctly and have some type of ongoing accounting and auditing system.

The levels of principal involvement in finance vary based on the districts of employment. Nevertheless, it is important for principals to be aware of relevant issues. The bottom line is that principals inherit tremendous fiduciary responsibilities by virtue of their positions. Principals must thus possess sufficient skill, knowledge, and dispositions, to exercise this responsibility in the best interest of their schools and stakeholders.

## Recommendations

It is important for principals to be aware of how state funding formulas function, were developed, and how they may have been altered through litigation. This information provides principals with an overview of school funding because it plays such an important role in their professional lives. As such, it would be helpful for principals to have concrete ideas about how to implement financial plans and procedures in their buildings and to best manage available resources. Thus, in light of their knowledge of school finance as it applies to their buildings, principals should consider the following recommendations regarding financial management:

1. Principals should meet regularly with their district school business managers and/or treasurers in order to keep apprised of current financial issues affecting their districts.
2. Principals shall create building-level finance committees to help in decision-making as to acquisition and allocation of financial resources.
3. Principals, along with stakeholders, should establish short- and long-term goals geared toward accomplishing goals, missions, and visions of both the district and the building. Principals and building financial committee members should review goals in order to ascertain progress.
4. Principals, in conjunction with building finance committees, should prioritize program needs and determine where expenditures will make the biggest difference for teaching and learning.
5. Principals should become adept at developing and maintaining accurate and up-to-date financial records. Recording both receipts and expenditures, as well as any additional, required paperwork, is essential.
6. Principals should require cash received to be deposited in appropriate bank accounts as soon as possible in accordance with board policy and state law.
7. Principals should keep up to date on both current and new issues related to educational finance. New requirements, new programs, and new equipment and materials can all call for additional expenditures. As such,

principals must actively seek professional development opportunities for themselves through workshops, seminars, graduate classes, online resources, and peer networking in order to remain current professionally.

8. Principals must also provide professional development opportunities for teachers and staff to keep them informed and up-to-date regarding their financial responsibilities. Teachers should understand procedures related to purchase orders as well as handling money generated through activities such as school clubs and fundraisers. Further, because noncertified office personal typically handle most financial transactions, they should fully understand their duties and responsibilities when it comes to handling money.

9. Principals may wish to create suggestion boxes to allow staff to make budgetary requests anonymously. This encourages input and will encourage less vocal faculty and staff to have a voice in fiscal issues.

10. Principals should review budgets at the end of school years in preparation for evaluating and developing next year's budget.

Adherence to the ten recommendations shown in the chapter can assist principals in successfully managing their buildings as well as fulfilling their financial fiduciary responsibilities entrusted to them by stakeholders

## CONCLUSION

Principals must accomplish a variety of tasks and responsibilities if they are to be successful in their professions. In addition to serving as visionary, instructional leaders, capable of facilitating changes leading to school improvement, they must also be adept at management activities. One of the most important management function principals must demonstrate deals with school finance.

How involved principals will be in finance depends on the districts of employment. Regardless of how much time principals are required to spend on school financial management, it is important that they have sufficient levels of understanding regarding how financial resources are acquired, expended, accounted, and audited. This is not only a component of good management, but it is also a matter of executing legal and ethical behaviors essential to being a good principal (Cooper and Speakman, 2004).

## REFERENCES

Brimley, V., & Garfield, R. R. (2008). *Financing education in a climate of change* (10th ed.). Boston, MA: Pearson Allyn and Bacon.

Carey, K. (November 7, 2002). *Overview of K-12 education finance.* Center on Budget and Policy Priorities. Available at http://www.cbpp.org/archives/11-7-02sfp2.htm.

Cooper, B. S., & Speakman, S. T. (2004). "The Three R's of Education Finance Reform: Re-Thinking, Re-Tooling, and Re-Evaluating School-Site Information." *Journal of Education Finance, 22*(4), pp. 337–367.

Drake, T. L., & Roe, W. (1994). *The principalship* (4th ed.). New York: Macmillan.

Every Student Succeeds Act, 20 U.S.C.A. §§6301 *et seq.* (2015).

FederalGrants.com (2016). *Block grants.* Available at http://www.federalgrants.com/block-grants.html.

Giles, C., Johnson, L., Brooks, S., & Jacobson, S. L. (2005). Building bridges, building community: Transformational leadership in a challenging urban context. *Journal of School Leadership, 15*(5), pp. 519–45.

Hadderman, M. (1999). *School-based budgeting, ERIC Digest Number 131.* Eric website. Available at http://files.eric.ed.gov/fulltext/ED434401.pdf.

Herman, J. J., & Herman, J. L. (1997). *School-based budgets: Getting, spending and accounting.* Lancaster, PA: Technomic Publishing.

Individuals with Disabilities Education Act, 20 U.S.C.A. §§1400 *et seq.* (2005).

Kessler, S., Snodgrass, A., & Davis, A. (2015). *The principal's survival guide.* Minneapolis, MN: Free Spirit Publishing.

Kowalski, T. J. (2010). *The school principal: Visionary leadership and competent management.* New York, NY: Routledge.

Mich. Comp. Laws Ann. §388.1620 (1979).

Mutter, D. W., & Parker, P. J. (2004). *School money matters: A handbook for principals.* Alexandria, VA: ASCD.

National Policy Board for Educational Administration, (NPBEA). (November 2011). *Educational leadership program recognition standards: Building level for institutions undergoing NCATE accreditation and ELCC program review.* Available at http://www.npbea.org/wp/wp-content/uploads/2015/06/ELCC-Building-Level-Standards-2011.pdf.

Legislative Service Commission. (2015). *School funding complete resource.* Available at from http://www.lsc.ohio.gov/schoolfunding/edufeb2015.pdf.

Odden, A. R., & Picus, L. O. (2014). *School finance: A policy perspective* (5th ed.). New York: McGraw Hill.

Odden, A. R., Wohlstetter, P., & Odden, E. (1995). Key issues in effective site-based management. (Report No. EJ506499). *School Business Affairs, 61*(5), pp. 4–12, 14, 16.

Ohio Revised Code, §117: 11, 2013 (2016).

Owings, W. A., & Kaplan, L. S. (2006). *American public school finance.* Belmont, CA: Thomas Wadsworth.

Ray, J. R., Candoli, I. C., & Hack, W. G. (2005). *School business administration: A planning approach* (8th ed.). Boston, MA: Pearson.

Rennie Center for Education Research & Policy. (2012). *Smart school budgeting: Resources for districts.* Cambridge, MA: Rennie Center for Education Research & Policy. Available at http://www.renniecenter.org/research/SmartSchoolBudgeting.pdf.

*Robinson v. Cahill,* 303 A.2d 273 (N. J. 1973).

*Rose v. Council for Better Education,* 790 S.W.2d 186 Ky (1989).

Russo, C. J. (1994–1995). School based decision making in Kentucky: Dawn of a new era or nothing new under the sun? *Kentucky Law Journal, 83*(1), pp. 123–56.

*San Antonio v. Rodriguez*, 411 U.S. 1 (1973).

*Serrano v. Priest* (I), 487 P. 2d 1241 (Cal. 1971).

*Serrano v. Priest* (II), 557 P.2d 929 (Cal. 1976).

Smith, J., Gasparian, H., Perry, N., & Capinpin, F. (2013, November 18). *Categorical funds: The intersection of school finance and governance.* Center for American Progress website. Available at https://www.americanprogress.org/issues/education/reports /2013/11/18/79510/categorical-funds-the-intersection-of-school-finance-and-governance/.

Stringer, P., & Hourani, R. B. (2013). Home–school relationships: A school management perspective. *Educational Research for Policy and Practice, 12*(2), pp. 149–74. doi: 10.1007/s10671-012-9134-0.

Thompson, D. C., & Wood, R. C. (2005). *Money and schools* (3rd ed.). Larchmont, NY: Eye on Education.

Thro, W. E. (2013). School finance litigation in *Key legal issues for schools* (2nd ed., pp. 45–56) C. J. Russo, Ed. Lanham, MD: Rowman & Littlefield Education.

U.S. Department of Education. (2015). *Every Student Succeeds Act (ESSA).* Available at http://www.ed.gov/essa?src=ft.

U. S. Department of Education. (2016). *The federal role in education.* Available at http://www2.ed.gov/about/overview/fed/role.html.

White, P. A. (1989). An overview of school based management: What does the research say? *NASSP Bulletin, 73*, pp. 1–8. doi: 10.1177/019263658907351802.

Wissler, D. F., & Ortiz, F. I. (1986). The decentralization process of school systems: A review of the literature. *Urban Education, 21*(3), pp. 280–94.

WordPress.com. (June 18, 2012). *Rose v CBE*: Significance to policies and procedures [Web log post]. Available at https://schoollawfinance.wordpress.com/court-cases/court-case-2/significance-to-policies-procedures/.

*Chapter 12*

# The Way Forward

## *It Is Now for All of Us*

### Bruce S. Cooper and Stephen Coffin

The way forward, now, begins—as we have shown—with adequate school funding, based on careful ways of determining the needs and best uses of school financial resources to carry out a school's mission. This book has pointed the way and has given some of the means and methods to make schools financially workable and educationally effective. But like other school reforms, quality education depends on quality resources and effective spending, now. Already, organizations are publishing the "goals for the new year, the next year." These include the following six steps to each our goals.

## SIX SUMMARY STEPS FOR EDUCATIONAL LEADERS

1. **Provide Equity and Opportunity for All Students—Regardless of Their Needs or Abilities:** Recall that education is critical to everyone, regardless of background or income; and overcoming the effects of poverty often depends on the school and the quality of education therein. Education is vital to students, families, society, and our nation. As we discussed in chapter 2, equitable education means raising enough funding, distributing it equally, effectively, and consistently. As one argument goes:

   Educational equity is dependent on two main factors. The first is *fairness*, which implies that factors specific to one's personal conditions should not interfere with the potential of academic success. The second important factor is *inclusion*, which refers to a comprehensive standard that applies to everyone in a certain education system. These two factors are closely related and are dependent on each other for true academic success of an educational system. ("Key Steps to Equity in Education" (PDF) Oecd.org.)

2. **Expand Support for Teachers and School Leaders:** Money matters, and so do leaders and teachers, communities, and school neighborhood.
3. **Improve Access, Affordability, and Student Outcomes in Postsecondary Education.**
4. **Promote Greater Use of Evidence and Data:** School leaders and their staff should gather, analyze, and use flexible funding to meet the needs of all students.

## Equity for All

a. Cutting the Gordian Knot of the Public Education Funding Debate: Spend More versus Cut Spending
b. Optimal Budgetary Levels: What is optimal? For what type of school or district?
c. Recommendations
d. Policy Implications, and
e. Forecasting the Future

## Conclusion and the Future

This book points the way, for school leaders and teachers, to understand the financing of their schools: the funding sources, uses, and importance of dollars for programs, and how to be effective in funding schools. We have reviewed the sources of funding—both public and private—the uses of funds, and their effectiveness in schools. We review and summarize the process in this final chapter, in the following steps:

1. **Know Funding Sources:** Money for education comes from many levels and sources. Put them together and raise the money that is available and the leaders' due.
2. **Build Strong Goals and Purposes, with Funding:** Keep eyes and ears open and stay alert to program opportunities and other sources of funding.
3. **Use Funds Effectively and Equitably (see chapter 2 above on the 4 E-word), so Students and Groups Are Not Excluded or Underfunded.** Take a constant and close look to see that funds are spent where needed and equitably.
4. **Look Public and Private:** Money, money everywhere; check both public federal state, and local funding sources, and private funds from local and state, and even national organizations.
5. **Track Dollars to the Kids:** We have built and patented a system for "tracking dollars to classrooms and kids" Cooper, Bruce S. & Speakman,

Sheree T. (1997). Called the Finance Analysis Model (FAM) and In-$ite, the method takes dollars at the system/district level, and follows the resources from the "central office" to the classroom, from the superintendents' level to the classrooms to the teachers and the students. FAM is a patented system for doing the following:

> An advanced software package for cost accounting and analysis, management reporting, performance assessment and decision support tool is described. The IN$ITE™ software package collects, organizes, manages and consolidates financial data and permits the standardized evaluation and comparison of different educational institutions. The software package implements the Finance Analysis Model For Education as a relational database for the efficient and cost-effective management of educational institutions.

When first developed in New York City, for Mayor Giuliani in 2003, In$ite found that only 21 percent of the enormous funding actually reached the classrooms, teachers, and kids. So much of the funds were spent on "Administration" including the offices, superintendents, and staffing for thirty-one community school boards in the city. *Driving bucks to the kids* is essential and involves teachers, guidance, aides, and other staff; books and materials; equipment and computers.

## MAKING MONEY MATTER MORE IN SCHOOLS, NOW!

Bernard Avishai's (2015) diagnoses of U.S. education are as valid as his prescriptions are naïve. He believes that education can work on all situations for all students. Although he grasps the troubles in our cities, the poor performance of our students, and the need for modernization, Avishai ignores three critical conditions confounding the innovations that he prefers. What is business's responsibility in educating students in the future?

First, he overlooks the *social context* of schooling. The breakup of family and the breakdown of community, together, adversely affect the ability of children to learn.

Second, public schools—fractured, overly specialized, and "loosely coupled" institutions—*are not set up or structured for easy reform.* Try introducing a new computerized mathematics program into a system where teachers work in isolated classrooms, away from other colleagues, and have little or no time to share with and support one another.

And third, public education is a *public monopoly*—and thus has hardly any incentives to innovate at all. Public education was until recently insulated from pressures to compete, change, and improve.

## CONCLUSION

Bernard Avishai and other reformers should consider many kinds of K-12 schools: public (magnet schools of choice), private, and parochial.

Because, as Cooper (1994a) argues in the *Harvard Business Review*, Avishai ignores these conditions—and, thus, we could fall into three traps as we finance our schools, as follows:

*1. The major problem is social, not technical.* For seventy-five years, critics of schools have concentrated on the *technical* side of the problem: for example, the use of space, time, technology, and *testing*. In fact, the failure of urban schools mostly results from a breakdown of the social and moral orders, including family, community, church, and school. When 65 percent of the live births in the District of Columbia, for example, are to single, minority mothers under the age of seventeen, the family as we know it has changed. Many of these children from single-parent homes arrive at school ill-prepared.

Avishai seems unaware of the need for *social stability* to make innovations work. How, one wonders, will advanced methods operate in schools, communities, and families that are in chaos? And for some reason, his solutions concentrate almost exclusively on public education, while private and parochial schools seem to work because of their high social capital, strict rules of conduct, and fundamental stability—conditions that are prevalent in traditional homes and communities.

*2. School structures resist change.* Urban school systems are difficult to change because they are such complex, underfunded, and isolated organizations. Pupils and their classes are usually divided by age, grade, ability, needs, subjects, interests, and location—reflecting the ideology of the very bureaucracies that Avishai predicts is vanishing. But, according to Avishai, the modern corporation is being "flattened," opened up, and made free, resembling a small entrepreneurial organization more than a corporate giant.

Mindless work is being performed by "brilliant" computers, freeing humans to do the "zestful" activities associated with new "intelligent enterprises," to use James Brian Quinn's term. However, while new business enterprises are undergoing a revolution, many schools are not—and their structure is greatly to blame for their inability to change.

*3. Public monopolies resist change.* Why, one wonders, would public school teachers and administrators even attempt all these radical changes? Adam Smith, of all people, would understand the limits of public monopolies. Without real competition and help, agencies have no incentive to change procedures, merge, and alter roles, and update, much less eliminate, divisions of labor.

Visits to school classrooms are informative. One sees teachers still keeping students' attendance and performance data in "roll books" and not on networked electronic systems. One finds a few old, often useless computers thrown in a corner, and students sitting and staring at teachers—not working and learning at computers. Learning is didactic, not interactive. And students continue to work alone instead of in groups around two-way "tele-computers" linked to "spectrum-infinite fiber-networks."

As everyone becomes a lifelong learner, *education*—including its full funding—is indeed critical. But what should business do? It makes little sense, as Adam Smith himself would warn, to have private corporations invest exclusively in public school monopolies. "It makes little sense, as Adam Smith himself would warn, to have private corporations invest exclusively in public school monopolies" (Shute & Cooper, 2015, p. 45).

Instead, communities should make a compact, first, to see that public, private, and parochial schools are available for all children, including the inner-city poor. Second, businesses should extend the compact to help the education of children, not to bankroll more overhead. Innovations that make schools more "thinking," problem-solving, cooperative organizations for children should be expanded.

Third, communities should concentrate on reforms that improve the structure of individual schools, much as business itself is being reorganized. After all, if public schools themselves are dull, repetitive places, how can education inspire students, much less help business?

Bernard Avishai (2014) is correct that today's learning organizations must become teaching organizations. With *business's* help, schools can learn—as they teach as well. Otherwise, we are all in trouble. And money matters, as improved schools require a smart use of funds, better budgeting, and careful, well-funded, and managed school programs. Now, these methods, and this book, provide the background, skills, and methods for school leaders. Use them, as school leaders are most important, critical managers of school funding, budgets, staffing, and programs—and leaders of excellent education of our children, now and in the future.

For as Bonstingl (1992) explains:

Suddenly, it seems, the name of W. Edwards Deming is everywhere. From relative obscurity in this country a dozen years ago, Deming's name has become synonymous with the movement he calls Quality Management, better known as TQM or Total Quality Management (TQM). This movement is spawning a new American revolution, as *quality* becomes our watchword in every aspect of life. TQM principles and practices are revitalizing businesses, government agencies, hospitals, social organizations, home life—and our own world of education.

# REFERENCES

Avishai, Bernard (April 2, 2012). "Real Life, Not "Counter-life." *The Daily Beast.* Retrieved August 12, 2015.

Bonstingl, J. J. (1992). The quality revolution in education. *Improving School Quality, 50*(3), p. 4.

Cooper, Bruce S. (1994a). Educating the workforce of the future and understanding Bernard Avishai. *Harvard Business Review. Special Issue: Developing Employees of the Future* (issue authors: Richard Riley, Sandra Feldman, Sofie Sa, Bruce S. Cooper, Diana Wyllie Rigden, Ted Kolderie, Hans Decker, G. Alfred Hess, Jr., and Allyson Tucker) (March–April), pp. 41–45.

Cooper, Bruce S. (1994b). Making money matter in education: A micro-financial model for determining school-level allocations, efficiency, and productivity. *Journal of Education Finance, 20* (Bruce S. Cooper, Robert Sarrel, Peter Dwarves, Frank Alfaro, Eddie Meier, Judith Samuels, & Susan Heinbuch) (March–April), pp. 66–87.

Cooper, B. S., & Speakman, S. T. (1997). The three R's of education finance reform: Re-thinking, re-tooling, and re-evaluating school-site information. *Journal of Education Finance, 22*(4), pp. 337–367.

Shute, J., & Cooper, B. S. (2015). *Fixing truancy now: Inviting students back to class.* Lanham, MD: Rowman & Littlefield.

# Editors

**Stephen Coffin** is a PhD candidate in education at the Graduate School of Education, Rutgers University, New Jersey, USA; teaches school finance as an adjunct professor at the Graduate Schools of Education for Montclair State University and Rutgers University; teaches school and higher education finance and economics for the Fordham University Graduate School of Education; serves on three editorial review boards; publishes articles, reports, chapters, and books; is a former school business administrator; has earned an MBA in finance and MPA in public administration; and focuses his research on education finance and policy, charter schools, community economic development, school business administration, school choice, and equal educational opportunity and equity.

**Bruce S. Cooper,** PhD, is Professor Emeritus, Education Administration and Public Policy, Graduate School of Education, Fordham University, New York. He also taught at University of Pennsylvania and Dartmouth College, after receiving his doctorate from the University of Chicago with Donald A. Erickson, as his mentor. Cooper has written forty-five books on education politics and policy, including *The Handbook of Education Politics and Policy,* in two editions with Lance D. Fusarelli and James Cibulka. He served as president of the Politics of Education Association and was a founding member of Private School Research Association. He received the Jay D. Scribner Award for Mentoring from the University Council of Education Administration (UCEA).

**David Dolph,** Ph.D. is a former school principal and superintendent. He is currently chair of the Department of Educational Administration at the University of Dayton.

**William Hartman** is Professor Emeritus, College of Education, The Pennsylvania State University, where he specialized in school finance and budgeting, fiscal modeling, and special education funding. He is currently President of Educational Finance Decisions, an educational consulting firm focused on budgeting, planning, and technical assistance for local school districts and state education agencies.

**Philip Nisonoff,** Assistant Superintendent of Schools/School Business Administrator Emerson Public Schools, Second Vice-President NJASBO. Today, more than any other time in the development of the American Educational System, our country's future depends on leadership to make sound financial decisions. Sound School Finance for Educational Excellence provides current leaders and aspiring leaders with a concise, well designed resource that will demystify the complex realm of the economic aspects financing our schools.

**Lawrence O. Picus** is professor of educational policy and finance at the University of Southern California Rossier School of Education. His research interests focus on adequacy and equity in school finance as well as efficiency and productivity in the provision of educational programs for PreK-12 school children. Picus is co-Author (with Allan R. Odden) of School Finance: A Policy Perspective, 5th edition. He is past-president of the Association for Education Finance and Policy, and past President of EdSource where he served as a member of the Board of Directors for 14 years.

**Charles J. Russo,** M. Div., J.D., Ed. D., is the Joseph Panzer Chair in Education in the School of Education and Health Services, Director of its Ph.D. Program, and Research Professor in the School of Law at the University of Dayton. As author or co-author of more than 280 articles in peer-reviewed journals; author, co-author, editor, or co-editor of 62 books, and more than 1,000 publications, he has spoken extensively on issues in Education Law in the United States and in twenty-nine other Nations.

**Robert Schoch** spent over 30 years as the business administrator in several of the largest school districts in Pennsylvania. He is now working with state declared financially distressed school systems developing and implementing financial recovery plans.